“Verna M. Linzey’s book is [illegible] convictions on baptism in t[illegible] and speaking in tongues, with the same ingenuousness and fervour which lit the flame of Pentecostalism one hundred years ago.”

—James D. G. Dunn, D.D.
Emeritus Professor, University of Durham

THE BAPTISM WITH THE HOLY SPIRIT

The reception of the Holy Spirit as confirmed by speaking in tongues

Verna M. Linzey, D.D.

Foreword by
Russell P. Spittler, Ph.D.
Provost Emeritus and Senior Professor of New Testament
Fuller Theological Seminary

The Baptism with the Holy Spirit

Verna M. Linzey, D.D.

The Baptism with the Holy Spirit explores the biblical and theological foundations of the experience known as the baptism with the Holy Spirit or the reception of the Holy Spirit as confirmed by speaking in tongues. In the process of explaining the experience, the book relies heavily on biblical resources. Thus, the presentation comes both from personal experience and from biblical research.

The variety of discussion is significant, moving from the nature of the Holy Spirit Himself through the experience of the baptism with the Holy Spirit, and explaining speaking in tongues. The book then shows the workings of the baptism and speaking in tongues through the Old and New Testaments. Finally, the chapters on how to receive the Holy Spirit and the necessity and results of receiving the Holy Spirit baptism add the practical application that will apply to everyone.

The Baptism with the Holy Spirit
by Verna M. Linzey, D.D.

Printed in the United States of America

ISBN 1-594670-59-5

Xulon Press
www.XulonPress.com

Xulon Press books are available in bookstores everywhere, and on the Web at www.XulonPress.com.

COMMENTS

"Verna Linzey's book is a restatement of classic Pentecostal convictions on baptism in the Spirit and speaking in tongues, with the same ingenuousness and fervour which lit the flame of Pentecostalism one hundred years ago."

Emeritus Professor James D. G. Dunn, DD
Department of Theology
University of Durham
United Kingdom

"In *The Baptism with the Holy Spirit*, Verna Linzey has given this generation a fresh new look at the Pentecostal experience as experienced by millions of people worldwide in the last century. With sound Biblical and historical insights, she offers the reader a clear roadmap to experience the power and gifts of the Holy Spirit today. I highly recommend it."

Vinson Synan, Ph.D.
Dean and Professor of Divinity
School of Divinity, Regent University
United States

"Verna Linzey has written a useful guide for any who may wish to know more about the Pentecostal teaching and experience of Baptism with the Holy Spirit."

William M. Menzies, Ph.D.
Chancellor, Asia Pacific Theological Seminary
Editor, Asian Journal of Pentecostal Studies
Philippines

"Verna M. Linzey's book on the baptism in the Holy Spirit is a delight to read. One will find in its pages many popular voices from among Evangelicals and Pentecostals of the past, quoted in support of an exposition that is broadly biblical, Christ centered, and relevant to contemporary Christian experience. I highly recommend it to lay people seeking a clear restatement of the classical Pentecostal understanding of Spirit baptism and its relationship to speaking in tongues."

Frank D. Macchia, D.Theol., Editor,
Pneuma: The Journal of the Society for Pentecostal Studies
Director of Graduate Program in Religion
Vanguard University of Southern California
United States

"This is a new and creative exposition of the biblical theology of the baptism with the Holy Spirit as believed and taught by the author, an Assemblies of God minister for over fifty years. As such, Dr. Linzey represents adequately the theology of the majority of classical Pentecostals (especially in North America), and there are no hidden surprises or controversies for them here. The author sets out to prove clearly the two distinctive classical Pentecostal positions of subsequence (that the baptism in the Spirit is a definite experience subsequent to conversion) and that of consequence (that the "primary" or "initial" evidence of Spirit baptism is speaking in tongues). This she does by tracing the experiences of the Holy Spirit throughout the Bible, leaving no stone unturned. And yet she writes for ordinary Christians in a manner easy to understand without polemical ire or attempt to enter into the raging debates in the wider Christian world. I heartily commend this as a well written, gentle and thoroughly biblical rather than primarily an academic book that will interest any who want to understand the central doctrine of classical Pentecostalism."

Allan Anderson, D.Th.
Programme Leader, Postgraduate Pentecostal Studies
Graduate Institute of Theology and Religion
University of Birmingham
United Kingdom

"Speaking in tongues is the most conspicuous sign of the baptism with the Holy Spirit for the authentic Pentecostal faith. This wonderful masterpiece deals extensively and in depth with the subject of the person and ministry of the Holy Spirit on the biblical, practical and pastoral level. This work is an incomparable treasure to the genuine Pentecostal experience, in which what is written in the Bible becomes the foundation of the Christian doctrines and the milestone of our Christian life."

Dr. Samhwan Kim, Pastor, Yoido Full Gospel Church
Director, International Theological Institute
South Korea

"As Pentecostals have become less Pentecostal in their understanding and practice, Dr. Verna M. Linzey's book provides not only a clear presentation of the baptism in the Spirit, the bed-rock belief of Pentecostalism, but helps the Pentecostals to be more informed and practicing Pentecostals. The book is reader-friendly in its plain language and with its practical side of the book. May the Pentecostals become more Pentecostal through the revival of the spiritual baptism, and for this prayer, this is an excellent book "for the rest of us!"

Wonsuk Ma, Ph.D.
Academic Dean, Asia Pacific Theological Seminary
Associate Editor, Asian Journal of Pentecostal Studies
Philippines

"A helpful, comprehensive, Bible-based discussion of what it means to be baptized in the Holy Spirit. I highly recommend this book to those who are searching for a more meaningful relationship with God, and those believers who want to know more about the names and work of the Holy Spirit throughout the Scriptures."

David G. Clark, Ph.D., Chair
Department of Biblical Studies
Professor of New Testament and Greek
Vanguard University of Southern California
United States

"Dr. Verna M. Linzey's *The Baptism with the Holy Spirit* presents a thorough and unique balance between scholarly research and genuine Pentecostal experience. I especially recommend Dr. Linzey's practical instructions on how to receive the Holy Spirit. Every Christian who wants to enjoy the fullness of joy and power in the Holy Spirit must read this book!"

Máximo Rossi, Jr., Ph.D., President
Bethany College
United States

"Dr. Verna M. Linzey helps you discover the secret of living beyond normal human limits by tapping into the power of God through the Holy Spirit. This stimulating and practical book explores this theme in depth, writing in a popular lively style which will enable many to understand and apply this vital teaching. This mighty weapon of spiritual warfare holds the secret to a life of miracles. I am praising God that I am blessed to read this book. I wish and pray that Dr. Linzey will be used like a guiding star to the Nations."

G. Joseph Daniel, Ph.D., President
International Nehemia Theological Seminary
India

"Verna Linzey stresses the importance of both believing in and experiencing the baptism with the Holy Spirit accompanied by the biblical evidence of speaking with tongues. I welcome this timely book on a vital topic."

David Petts, Ph.D., Principal
Mattersey Hall Bible College
United Kingdom

"Dr. Verna Linzey has written the most complete book on the Baptism with the Holy Spirit. It has been my pleasure to read it. A must read for all serious students of the Word."

Benjamin L. Thornley, D.D., Vice President
Kingsway Christian College and Theological Seminary
United States

"Dr. Verna M. Linzey has produced a clear and succinct treatise on the Pentecostal doctrine of Spirit baptism. Her work is clearly defined and easy to read. Dr. Linzey is to be commended for her work, for she has provided Pentecostal pastors and leaders of discipleship programmes a functional manual, which can be safely put into the hands of young Christians who are seeking the Baptism in the Spirit."

Pastor David Carnduff, M.Th., Principal
Irish Pentecostal Bible College
United Kingdom

"From a little Bible school in Kansas and a humble mission in California, the Pentecostal revival has literally changed the world. Any book which is Biblically sound and spiritually practical while addressing that Pentecostal revival will be of great help to any person of God. Dr. Verna M. Linzey's *The Baptism with the Holy Spirit* is such a book."

Don Meyer, Ph.D., President
Valley Forge Christian College
United States

"*The Baptism with the Holy Spirit* is a timely, carefully researched and full explanation of the classical Pentecostal position on the subject. Dr. Verna M. Linzey combines her vast knowledge of Biblical exposition and her warm-hearted pastoral experience to bring us a masterful and unique presentation. She accurately portrays the Pentecostal contribution to a Biblical understanding of Baptism with the Spirit and her treatment of the issues of 'subsequence' and 'tongues' is particularly helpful. This book is a must for all Pastors and lay people who want to understand and experience the work of the Holy Spirit today."

Dr. Colin Dye, Senior Pastor
Kensington Temple, London City Church
United Kingdom

"Dr. Verna M. Linzey writes to share from many decades of living and walking under the anointing that comes with "The Baptism with the Holy Spirit." She has experienced what she herewith teaches, what any Bible-believing person should see as proof – that 'Jesus is the same yesterday, today and forever' with signs and wonders for all time on planet earth."

Chaplain, Colonel Jim Ammerman, USA (Ret.)
President and Founder, Chaplaincy Full Gospel Churches

"A masterful, biblical, and personal description of the Holy Spirit's historical and present activity! Dr. Linzey gives exactitude on this subject which helps the Christian to have discernment between the Holy Spirit's activity and self promoted emotionalism. The research is rounded and complete. Dr. Linzey's work is a 'must read' for every serious Christian!"

Stephen Houston, D.D., Senior Pastor
World Faith Center, Dallas, Texas

"*The Baptism with the Holy Spirit* by Dr. Verna Linzey is ecumenically relevant and based on academic research."

Rear Admiral Bennett S. Sparks, USCG (Ret.)
Former National President,
Reserve Officers' Association of the United States

"I have just finished reading Dr. Verna Linzey's book. I highly recommend this book for spiritual inspiration and guidance!"

The Honorable Lori Holt Pfeiler
Mayor of Escondido, California

"Dr. Linzey's book is a powerful and scripturally accurate statement on the importance of the Holy Spirit Baptism in the life of both the individual believer and the church. In our world of declining moral standards, an emphasis on the need of Spirit–filled believers is vital. This timely book meets a need of the worldwide 21st century church."

Rev. Robert B. Turnbull
Former Director International Ministries
Christian Broadcasting Network

DEDICATION

To Jesus Christ, my best friend,
who died for me so that I may have eternal life.
He said in John 15:13, "Greater love has no one than this,
that he lay down his life for his friends."
So, in dedication to Christ I have written this hymn:

O Blessed Jesus

O blessed Jesus, my precious Savior
He came from Heaven to die for me.
He was resurrected and went to glory
He promised to come again for me.

It may be evening, it may be morning
He'll guide us to that peaceful shore.
He'll take us with Him to dwell in Heaven
O what a gathering to part no more!

- Verna M. Linzey -

~~~~~~~~~~~~~~~~~~~~~~
~~~~~~~~~~~~~~~~~~~~~~

TABLE OF CONTENTS

PREFACE

One Sunday morning in December of 1941, the son of a Rabbi was visiting San Diego from New York. The young Jewish man had nothing to do on Sunday since most businesses were closed. So he got up, got dressed, and took a walk. He was standing near a corner when the First Assembly of God Sunday School bus stopped and some people including children got on the bus. He got on the same bus to see where the bus would take them. The bus took them to the church on 6th and Fir streets. So he went in the church with the other people and attended the morning service.

During the service a little lady stood up and spoke in tongues (in a language unknown to her). It was perfect Hebrew. After the service, the Jewish man went up to the pastor and said he wanted to meet the little Hebrew lady who stood up during the service and addressed the congregation. Pastor E. E. Fullerton said, "We don't have a Hebrew lady here." The Jewish man said, "Yes, the lady that stood up and addressed the people during the service."

Pastor Fullerton said, "Oh, that was by the Holy Spirit—a gift—that she spoke." Pastor Fullerton took the Jewish man over and introduced him to the lady who had spoken in tongues. The Jewish man talked to her in Hebrew. She did not understand a word he said. So the pastor explained how what had happened was similar to the events on the Day of Pentecost in Acts chapter 2. It was an act of God and a moving of the Holy Spirit. The Jewish man gave his heart to God and accepted Christ into his life right then. Wednesday night he was back in church, and after receiving the baptism with the Holy Spirit as confirmed by speaking in tongues, he told the congregation he was going back to New York and tell his people about Jesus Christ. I witnessed this young man's experience.

This book explores the theological foundation for the baptism with the Holy Spirit. It also references the theological work on the Holy Spirit by many theologians, including Rev. P.C. Nelson who was the president of Southwestern Bible School in Enid, Oklahoma, which is now Southwestern Assemblies of God University in Waxahachie, Texas.

While growing up in Coffeyville, Kansas, the Nelsons would often stop by our house on their way back to Enid after taking faculty and students to churches in the region to minister. I never dreamed that I would eventually attend Southwestern Bible School. I would ask my mother if I could get up and sit around the table and listen to them talk about the Bible and prophecy or how people got saved or healed. I am grateful for the impact P.C. Nelson has made on my life.

I would like to acknowledge many gracious friends in my life who have been of real encouragement in the writing of this book. I would like to thank Russ Spittler for his tremendous support of this work. His encouragement provided validation to me personally that this manuscript needed to be written.

Frank Macchia has endeared himself to me by being available to analyze my work and its relevance to contemporary Christianity. His response to this work is affirming. Allan Anderson's feedback on the style of this work is very insightful and has provided a panoramic view of this work. His careful attention to the details and nuances of the intent and purpose of this work is most appreciated. I would like to thank Samhwan Kim for focusing on the value of this work to the foundation of the Pentecostal experience and its usefulness to pastors.

Wonsuk Ma rightly observes the fading of the Pentecostal experience among Pentecostals. I pray that this work rekindles the desire among believers to seek all that God has to offer. Dr. Ma exhibits servant-hood, a spirituality shown in encouraging our work for the Lord. I have seen this quality in his helpfulness to my endeavor as presented before you. Chaplain, Colonel Jim Ammerman has been very accommodating of my ministry, and his optimism toward this work has been greatly appreciated.

Dr. Ben Thornley has encouraged me in many ways in the ministry and shared many kind words to give me zeal to do more for God's kingdom. The Honorable Lori Holt Pfeiler has always been there for me with words of encouragement and recognition. My sweet cousins, Howard and Vera McCloud, have continually held me up in prayer. My youngest son, Chaplain, Major Jim Linzey, has also prayed much for me and gave me great encouragement to pursue writing this book. I am especially grateful to Shirley Felt, former Chairman of the Humanities Division of Vanguard University of Southern California, who edited and corrected the manuscript. She is also my dear friend who has prayed for this work.

My dear mother, the late Alice May Doyle, inspired me in my work for God and conveyed to me many times in her own special way that if I placed my abilities and gifts in God's hands, then God would use them according to His divine will. And most important, my faithful and caring husband for sixty-two years, Stanford E. Linzey, Jr., who has stood with me and supported me in prayer as I have completed this manuscript, has been there beside me all the time. I am grateful for the years of ministry together, learning together how to follow the leading of the Holy Spirit to best serve the Church.

This work stems from years of study, practical experience, and ministry on the field for our Lord Jesus Christ. May this book provide clarity on the doctrine of the baptism with the Holy Spirit and enable its readers to understand its eternal truths.

Verna M. Linzey
Escondido, California
August 2003

FOREWORD

For more than a half century, Verna Linzey and her husband, Stan Linzey, shared ministry in the Assemblies of God, one of the largest North American Pentecostal denominations. This service included worldwide travel while Stan Linzey for three decades served as a military chaplain. Verna Linzey, throughout these years, not only shared ministry: she also oversaw the lively and mobile family of ten children—many of whom themselves have entered the ministry as pastors, professors, and chaplains. Within the U. S. Navy Chaplain Corps, Stan Linzey gained an informal designation as the "father of the fleet"—which might warrant titling Verna Linzey as "the mother of the fleet."

The Linzeys have always represented a staunch classical Pentecostalism. They together have had a ministry that focused on leading folk to experience the distinctive Pentecostal experience known as the Baptism in the Holy Spirit. No wonder, then, that Verna Linzey writes on that topic.

Standing in the tradition of Frank Boyd, P. C. Nelson, and Ernest S. Williams, Verna Linzey presents in this book a fresh statement of the classical Pentecostal viewpoint on this overwhelming experience of the Spirit and its accompanying effect, speaking in tongues. Written for everyday Christians, this book does not aim to engage treatments of the subject done from lofty academic levels. Neither the text nor the bibliography of this work, for example, contains references to James Dunn's book *Baptism in the Holy Spirit* (Allenson, 1970) or to the technical academic debate that followed that work, or to Francis Martin's brief but able treatment, *Baptism in the Holy Spirit* (Franciscan University Press, 1986). (For such engagement, readers can turn to the newly emerging academic edges in Pentecostal scholarship, readily sampled in journals like *Pneuma: The Journal of the Society for Pentecostal Studies, The Journal of Pentecostal Theology,* or *JEPTA: The Journal of the European Pentecostal Theological Association.*)

Rather, this book presents non-technical Bible studies in a way that has regularly characterized the Pentecostal movement nearly from its beginning a century ago. But this book also includes what many similar works have not: pastoral counsel and practical advice for those seeking to receive, or to guide others toward receiving, the hallmark Pentecostal encounter with the Holy Spirit. The result is something of a new handbook for those interested in the Pentecostal experience. I commend the work to readers of every sort.

Russell P. Spittler, Ph.D.
Provost Emeritus and Senior Professor of New Testament
Fuller Theological Seminary
Pasadena, California
August 2003

INTRODUCTION

During the Battle of Midway in World War II, my husband, Stanford E. Linzey, Jr., was stationed on the *USS Yorktown*. The *Yorktown* was one of the aircraft carriers, with the *USS Enterprise* and *USS Hornet*, which ensured that the United States would win this battle. Saving Midway Island was the pivotal mission in winning the War on the Pacific front. The aircraft carriers sailed within 200 miles northeast of Midway to protect Midway from the attack of the Japanese fleet. As the ships sailed northwest toward their destination, a sense of fatal despair filled the *Yorktown*. Stan began to experience this tremendous fear of death. On June 3, 1942, Stan lay in his bunk in the dark praying, asking God to remove this fear. After some time in prayer, God instantly removed this fear and gave him a deep sense of relief and peace, no matter what would transpire from this battle.

I was back in San Diego and knew nothing of the *Yorktown's* impending disaster, the battle, or Stan's experience in prayer. But at this time, about 5,000 miles away from him, I felt a strange need to pray in the Spirit, not knowing why. I knelt on the floor by the bed and prayed in the Spirit. It was between five and six o'clock in the evening. After about an hour, I felt a release in my spirit and that God had answered my prayers. When Stan and I compared notes later, we found that we had united in prayer that same day as we continued by faith to be sensitive to the moving of the Holy Spirit. The *Yorktown* was subsequently bombed and torpedoed at Midway, but Stan survived and the battle was won.

One never knows when tragedy will strike our world, nation, or personal lives. So we must be vigilant and pray in the Spirit on all occasions. Jesus said in John 14:27, "Peace I leave with you; my peace I give you. I do not give to you as the world gives. Do not let your hearts be troubled and do not be afraid." Through praying in the Spirit, we may find ourselves in extraordinary leadership roles and contribute to the world's course of events in positive ways. We must live by faith, be led of the Spirit, and lead by example. Then God will release His Spirit in us to help us to be effective leaders as He wills in our spheres of influence in this world.

J. Gilchrist Lawson reports that "The Holy Spirit is mentioned over 400 times in the Bible under 41 different names and titles. One verse in 26 concerns the work of the Holy Spirit" (7). Certainly someone as important as that in the Holy Scriptures deserves our attention.

The work of the Holy Spirit in our dispensation belongs to the time span from Pentecost to the Second Coming of our Lord. The Holy Spirit's work will continue through eternity, but He is on a specific, definite mission right now. The Holy Spirit, according to George E. Holmes, came in a special way at an appointed time and is now fulfilling His mission on the earth. "When it is accomplished, He will ascend to heaven. This does not mean He will have no ministry in the ages to come but, like Christ, He is now fulfilling a specific mission that had a definite beginning and will have a recognized end" (15).

Richard E. Orchard, in "The Holy Spirit and This Age," says that the divine successor of Jesus—another coequal with Jesus himself—came into the world at Pentecost. He had been here before of course, but at Pentecost He came to take the place of our Lord's physical presence and be an abiding Comforter to the disciples. This one who replaced Jesus had an appointed ministry and an appointed time. Jesus said, "He [the Father] shall give you another comforter, that he may abide with you forever" (John 14:16). Thus, "the perpetuity of the presence of Jesus is guaranteed in the hearts of His disciples by the glorious ministry of His coequal, the Holy Spirit" (Orchard, 6). The present ministry of the Holy Spirit is to bring the beauty of Jesus into the lives of believers. Jesus tells us that the Holy Spirit "will guide you into all truth . . . He will tell you what is yet to come . . . He will bring glory to me by taking from what is mine and making it known to you" (John 16:13, 14).

We must remember that the ultimate purpose of God in redemption is not simply to get the sinner away from the consequences of sin, but the sinner's complete restoration to the image and likeness of God. We are saved to be sons, not just survivors (Lancaster, "Transforming Spirit," 22). We are called to be transformed into the image of Christ. And "for this we need the transforming power of the Holy Spirit, for without Him neither the desire to be like Christ nor the power to realize that likeness can be made possible" (Lancaster, 27).

The Holy Spirit is working in this time-span, this dispensation, to build a holy temple to the Lord, for "in him you too are being built together to become a dwelling in which God lives by His Spirit" (Eph. 2:22). He is building Christ into the lives of believers. He is transforming, regenerating, converting. He is tearing down the old and building the new. Orchard states that "As the Father revealed himself through the Son, so the Son by the Holy Spirit now reveals himself through the Church" (8). The Holy Spirit, then, is essential to the foundation of the New Testament Church.

The baptism with the Holy Spirit is not simply a way to feel good or to experience joy. This experience takes us into deeper communion with God. Such communion with God will certainly change us. We should be transformed into more dynamic Christians. We should hear God more clearly and be led by Him more fully.

The Holy Spirit of God came to His people on the Day of Pentecost as a rushing mighty wind and as flaming tongues of fire. From that day to this, He has been with His people. Sometimes we pray that the Holy Spirit may be poured out on us, but He is already with us. What we need is to appropriate the power of what He has already given us. God gives us no gift merely for our selfish luxury. The gift of the Holy Spirit is given to us for our power and for our use and not only for our personal gratification. Let us take the responsibility of the gift as well as the glory and joy that comes with the gift.

Verna M. Linzey
Escondido, California
August 2003

CHAPTER I

THE NATURE OF THE HOLY SPIRIT

Christians must recognize the Holy Spirit as a divine Person. He is neither an influence only nor just a different name for Jesus. He is a separate person of the Godhead. We know He is divine because Jesus associates the Holy Spirit with Himself and with the Father. The trinity is a whole, but it is certainly three separate persons as well. Frank Boyd makes a distinction for us of the different roles the Godhead takes. He explains that "The Father is the *fullness* of the Godhead *invisible* (John 1:18); the Son is the *fullness* of the Godhead *manifested* (John 1:14-18); the Spirit is all the *fullness* of the Godhead *acting immediately upon the creature* (I Cor. 2:9, 10)" (9, italics are Boyd's). The Holy Spirit, according to Arthur H. Parsons, in "The Personality of the Holy Spirit," is "the administrator of the affairs of grace in this dispensation" (8); and Jesus said "When he is come, he will reprove the world of sin, and of righteousness, and of judgment" (John 16:8).

Albert L. Hoy, in "The Spirit of Christ," points out that the New Testament gives several designations to the Holy Spirit, such as the Spirit of the Father (Matt. 10:20), the Spirit of Christ (Rom. 8:9), the Spirit of truth (John 14:17), the Spirit of holiness (Rom. 1:4), the Spirit of life (Rom. 8:2), the Spirit of adoption (Rom. 8:15), the Spirit of grace (Heb. 10:29), and the Spirit of glory (I Peter 4:14) (23). In fact, adds James R. McIntire in *The Life of the Holy Spirit,* in the New Testament more than 25 names are given the Holy Spirit, the more familiar ones being given to Him by Jesus (35). The name "The Holy Spirit" is given Him more than a hundred times. He is also called the Spirit of Truth, the Comforter, the Spirit of the Lord, the Spirit of your Father, the Spirit, the Spirit of God, the Spirit of Christ, the Spirit of His Son, the eternal Spirit, the Holy Spirit of God, the Spirit of Christ, the Spirit of adoption, the Spirit of holiness, the Spirit of life in Christ Jesus, and the Spirit of power (McIntire, 36).

Probably the most well-known name, though, is the *Paraclete* or Comforter, often translated as the Counselor or Advocate. Jesus said, "I will ask the Father, and he will give you another Counselor to be with you forever—the Spirit of Truth" (John 14:16). He is a personal helper. The Holy Spirit is the ever-present, ever-welcome, divine *Paraclete* (Comforter/Counselor). No English word adequately translates the Greek word "parakletos," according to A. L. Lastinger in "The *Parakletos*: Our Holy Ally," particularly in the Scripture where Jesus says "And I will ask the Father, and he will give you another [*Parakletos*] Counselor/Comforter to be with you forever—the Spirit of Truth" (John 14:16). The two Greek words which combine to form the term, *para* meaning "beside" and *kaleo* meaning "to call," result in the meaning "to call beside" (1). William Barclay, in *The Gospel of John*, explains that the word, though it was used in several ways, was always used of someone called in to help in time of trouble or need (qtd. in Lastinger, 2).

The context of the word indicates that Jesus was referring to himself as being the prior Comforter/Counselor and the Holy Spirit as being another Comforter/Counselor. The adjective *allos* means "another of the same sort"; so "another Comforter" means one of the same kind as the disciples had previously had in Jesus. In other words, the Holy Spirit was to be everything to believers that Jesus had been to the Disciples, for He was a Comforter of the same sort. Lastinger points out that the word *allos* is close to the origin of the English word "ally." And "an ally is one who certainly offers more than just moral support; he is willing to throw himself into the conflict and fight alongside his friend for the ultimate goal of victory. Your battle becomes his battle, your enemy, his enemy, and your need his need" (2). This is the kind of ally or Counselor Jesus left with us.

Most of us realize that the Holy Spirit is a Comforter or Counselor or Advocate because of what Jesus said to the Disciples: "When I go I will send another Comforter to you" (John 14:16). However, how much else do we know about the Holy Spirit? We have heard Him called the third person of the trinity, and He is. But so often the title Holy Spirit, or "Holy Ghost" as the King James Version translates, evokes in us images of ghost-likeness, or mystery, or unearthliness, or something intangible and out of the realm of real life. If we look carefully at Scripture, though, we see that the Holy Spirit is not an "it" but a Person; in fact He is just as much a person as God the Father and God the Son. He can be spoken against and sinned against (Matt. 12:31-32), He can be lied to (Acts 5:3), He can be provoked (Acts 5:9), He can be resisted (Acts 7:51), and He can be quenched (suppressed, stifled) (I Thess. 5:19). All of these are traits we would associate with a person. His ministries are those of a person too—he ministers love, joy, peace, hope. He is the executive member of the Godhead, the one who performs the will of the Father.

The coming of the Holy Spirit was essentially the out-breathing of God's own life. According to John Lancaster, in "The Life-Style of the Spirit," this out-breathing of God took place after the resurrection of Christ, so the breath or Spirit that Christ gave to the Disciples was the breath of Resurrection life. Resurrection life is divine life victorious over sin; it is a life that has come into contact with sin and triumphed over it. Jesus "communicates this [resurrection] life to us when He breathes the Holy Spirit into us . . . And the essential nature of that life is victorious holiness" (5). Holiness is the Holy Spirit's essential nature. His name bears witness of that fact: *Holy* Spirit. We are bound to assume, then, that the "church into which Christ has breathed His Holy Spirit will be outstanding for its holiness" (5). It is not possible for the church to live in holiness without being baptized with the Holy Spirit. The early church demanded holiness, not only in actions but also in motives. Witness the case of Simon the sorcerer (Acts 8:19-23); it wasn't enough that he would seek for the supernatural experience the disciples had, but Peter demanded that his motives in seeking it should glorify God as well (Lancaster, 7).

How does the Holy Spirit relate to the human personality? The human intellect is available for the Holy Spirit to use. The greatest truth in the world—the knowledge of the Kingdom of God and of Jesus Himself—will never be known except by those who have the Holy Spirit within them (see John 3:5) (Parsons, 8). The Holy Spirit illuminates the believer's mind (Ford, "Christian Growth" 9). Through the Holy Spirit believers are given unusual insight and understanding of the ways of God. I Cor. 2:10 tells us the Spirit knows the "deep things" of God and He enables our minds to grasp spiritual concepts. That kind of knowledge is not possible without His help.

The Holy Spirit has more than one function in our lives. Lastinger lists several ways the Holy Spirit can be depended on to function in the lives of believers. We are told that He will do the following and more for us. In John 14:26 He will teach all things and bring all things to our remembrance. The Holy Spirit will testify of Jesus (John 15:26). In John 16:8-11 He reproves the world of sin. In John 16:13 we are told that He will guide us into all truth. In John 16:14 we see that one of His ministries is to glorify Jesus. In Acts 10:19, 20 the Holy Spirit controls the movement of believers. In Acts 13:2 He directs in selection of the Early Church leaders. And in Romans 8:11 the Holy Spirit quickens our mortal bodies (Lastinger, "The Parakletos" 2).

What is the role of the Holy Spirit in the process of the Christian's spiritual growth? Romans 5:5 declares that "God has poured out his love into our hearts by the Holy Spirit whom He has given us." In other words, it is because of and through the Holy Spirit that we can experience the abundance of God's love at all. The Holy Spirit, when he fills the believer, brings an inner awareness of divine love. This love reaches from the believer toward God. The Holy Spirit, then, directs us to God in love, states Charles W. Ford, in "The Holy Spirit and Christian Growth" (8).

Ford also points out other ways the Holy Spirit is especially active in the Christian growth of all believers. The Holy Spirit helps us to bear witness of Christ; "you will receive power . . . and you will be witnesses to me" (Acts 1:8). Living in the Spirit leads us to pray according to the will of God. The Holy Spirit is omniscient; He knows all things. Therefore, He can give us the mind of God in prayer (Ford, 8). And also the Holy Spirit helps us in prayer (Rom.8:26). He puts the burden of prayer on the intercessor and then prays through the intercessor. The Holy Spirit can catch our inexpressible sighs, tears, unutterable desires and translate them into an intelligent petition (Parsons, 9). The key to spiritual growth is to be filled with the Holy Spirit and yield totally to Him (Ford, "Christian Growth," 9).

Jesus said the Holy Spirit would lead us into all truth. What is truth? Jesus answered this question in John 14:6: "I am the way, the truth, and the life." Jesus Christ is the embodiment of truth. To know who Jesus is, what He taught, and what He wants us to become should be our first goal. The Holy Spirit is the One who can lead us to know Christ. What the human mind is incapable of, the Holy Spirit can accomplish. The Holy Spirit helps us in the quest for truth (John 16:13). The Holy Spirit is the helper in the entire realm of truth. The Holy Spirit is the agent that leads us into Christ who alone is truth. "Truth is more than an opinion or a tradition but the personal involvement in the life of Christ himself" (Parsons, 9).

Clearly, then, we can see that the Holy Spirit is personally involved with every believer, every Christian. He brings us into relation with Christ in the first place, and then He has continuing ministry in our lives from the point of salvation onward. What are these areas of His involvement in the lives of all believers? We have already mentioned many parts of our lives where we expect and receive daily help from the Holy Spirit. However, Robert C. Frost, in *Set My Spirit Free* (37-39), gives a detailed list of many other ways we see the Holy Spirit operating, both in the times when the Scriptures were being lived and written and now in our everyday lives. Maybe a synopsis of some of these other ways the Holy Spirit is involved in our lives would be informative. Notice that the Holy Spirit

- Causes us to rest when we need it—Isa. 63:14
- Causes us to walk in God's ways—Ezek. 36:27
- Ministers life to us—Job 33:4, Rom. 8:11
- Pours Himself upon us—Joel 2:28, Acts 2:17-18

- Empowers the weak—Micah 3:8, Luke 24:49, Tim. 1:7
- Speaks to and through us—Matt. 10:20, Rev. 2:7, Rev. 22:17
- Teaches us—Luke 12:12, John 14:26
- Regenerates us—at our spiritual birth—Titus 3:5
- Testifies to us of Jesus—John 15:26
- Convicts the world of sin—John 16:8
- Guides us into all truth—John 16:13
- Gives divine utterance to those who pray in the Spirit—Acts 2:4, Eph. 6:18
- Gives boldness for us to witness—Acts 4:31
- Ordains and approves the servants of God—Acts 13:2-4
- Fills us with joy—I Thess. 1:6
- Intercedes for us—Rom. 8:26
- Justifies and Sanctifies each believer—I Cor. 6:11, II Thess. 2:13
- Indwells our lives—makes us temples of God—I Cor. 3:16, I Cor. 6:19
- Gives spiritual gifts to us—I Cor. 12:4-11
- Opposes the works of the flesh in our lives—Gal. 5:16-18
- Warns us about end-time deception—I Tim. 4:1
- Gives us power, love, and a sound mind—II Tim. 1:7
- Invites us to drink freely from the water of life—Rev. 22:17.

The function of the Holy Spirit is also seen in Titus 3:5: "he saved us . . . by the washing of regeneration and renewal in the Holy Spirit" (RSV). Both cleansing and renewal are functions of the Spirit. Believers, after conversion, need to be renewed in the image of God through spiritual consciousness. Without this operation of the Holy Spirit, the new birth will be abortive (Hoy, "Regeneration," 16). Now that the new believer has found salvation and been brought into the experience of the new birth, he can worship his newfound Redeemer through his own spirit meeting the Holy Spirit. "He who is united to the Lord becomes one spirit with him" (I Cor. 6:17 RSV).

However, it remains that the most important role of the Holy Spirit is to glorify Christ. Albert L. Hoy, in "The Spirit of Sonship," emphasizes the point that the main work of the Holy Spirit is to produce Christlikeness in believers. In fact, Jesus declared to His disciples that the prime purpose of the indwelling Spirit is to reveal Christ to the believer (John 15:26), and revealing Christ should result in the disciple becoming more like the Master. Before the Dispensation of Grace the work of the Holy Spirit in the saints of God was primarily to produce the Perfect man—Christ. The Old Testament prophets, then, have nothing to say about the Church—the bride of Christ. Their prophetic focus is on the character and authority of the Messiah, the Christ. But when the Messiah appeared, the purpose of the Spirit to produce the Perfect Man had been accomplished. Now the Spirit can direct His energies to create the Bride of the Perfect Man. "From the book of Acts onward, wherever the Holy Spirit is seen at work, he is gathering and refining the members of the bride of Christ" (12).

Jesus taught us to look for the Comforter's coming as an advance upon His own ministry. The Holy Spirit was to be a greater blessing to his people than Jesus' own personal companionship with them. How could this be? Ellis explains that "It is the Holy Spirit who gives spiritual life, quickens and sustains it, gives strength, implants hope, grants liberty; testifies to and glorifies the Christ; leads, guides, teaches, comforts, sanctifies, supports and sustains the believer" (137). Christ is the foundation of faith, and the Holy Spirit is the fountain of all spiritual life.

When Paul says to the Corinthians, "No eye has seen, no ear has heard, no mind has conceived what God has prepared for those who love him, but God has revealed it to us by his Spirit. The Spirit searches all things, even the deep things of God" (I Cor. 2:9, 10), we see the advantage, and the advance, that the Holy Spirit will have over and upon the physical ministry of Christ. According to Ellis, "The advent of the Holy Spirit is the final and most glorious manifestation of God that will be granted the world, or the Church, until his dispensation will be superseded by the Second Advent of our Lord as the 'King of Saints'" (138). A. J. Gordon adds, "The Spirit of God is the successor of the Son of God in His official ministry on earth. Until Christ's earthly work for His church had been finished, the Spirit's work in this world could not properly begin" (7, cited in Thomas 63).

CHAPTER II

WHAT IS THE BAPTISM WITH THE HOLY SPIRIT?

The Baptism with the Holy Spirit was planned by God. Over 400 years before the outpouring on the Day of Pentecost, the prophet Joel spoke of the event: "I will pour out my Spirit on all people" (Joel 2:28, 29). And 300 years before Joel, Isaiah prophesied the outpouring of the Holy Spirit: "The fortress will be abandoned . . . till the Spirit is poured upon us from on high" (Isa. 33:14-15).

Many people wonder why we use the term "baptism." David du Plessis, in *The Spirit Bade Me Go*, explains that God gave the word to John the Baptist when John told the people, "I baptize you with water for repentance. . . . He [Christ] will baptize you with the Holy Spirit and with fire" (Matt. 3:11). Further, John the Baptist stated that "the one who sent me to baptize with water told me, 'The man on whom you see the Spirit come down and remain is he who will baptize with the Holy Spirit'" (John 1:33). Jesus confirmed this statement when He said to the disciples, "For John baptized with water; but in a few days you will be baptized with the Holy Spirit" (Acts 1:5). Thus Christ began "His ministry of baptizing in the Holy Spirit on the day of Pentecost. This was the first time that any followers of Christ were baptized in the Holy Spirit by Him" (Du Plessis, 69).

F. M. Ellis, in his article "The Holy Spirit and the Christian," contends that such terms as "Baptized with the Holy Spirit," "The

Holy Spirit fell on them," "The Holy Spirit came," "Receive the Holy Spirit," "The power of the Holy Spirit," "The fellowship of the Holy Spirit" (p. 124) are applied to believers in Christ—not to people who are not believers. Consequently, we know that the Holy Spirit has a special, separate ministry to believers that does not apply to the unbeliever. He adds, "From the Christ, 'the organ of external revelation,' attention is being turned to the Holy Spirit—'the organ of internal revelation.' From the Advocate for us, who is with the Father, Christians are earnestly asking to know more of the advocate with us, who is here among us" (Ellis, 125). That Spirit within us comes with the baptism with the Holy Spirit.

The experience the disciples received on the Day of Pentecost—the same experience received by many thousands of believers since—is commonly called "the Baptism with the Holy Spirit." The definition of "the baptism with the Holy Spirit" is *the reception of the Holy Spirit as confirmed by speaking in tongues* (Linzey, 37). John the Baptist's prediction concerning Jesus was that "He will baptize you with the Holy Spirit and with fire" (Matt. 3:11). And Christ Himself verified the term when He promised the disciples, "You will be baptized with the Holy Spirit" (Acts 1:5). Again the term was verified in Acts 11:16 after its initial fulfillment in the second chapter of Acts.

However, the Scriptures do not limit themselves to a single term for that experience, notes Frank B. Rice, because there are several terms used even of that experience of the first Pentecost (7), for example these: "Baptized with the Holy Spirit" (Acts 1:5), "the Holy Spirit comes upon you" (1:8), "they were all filled with the Holy Spirit" (2:4), "I will pour out of my Spirit upon all people" (2:17), "the promised Holy Spirit . . . poured out" (2:33), "you will receive the gift of the Holy Spirit" (2:38) (Rice, 7).

That this one experience is designated many ways in the Bible, R. A. Torrey, in his book *The Baptism with the Holy Spirit*, verifies by pointing out the most important listings. In Acts 1:5 Jesus said, "You will be baptized with the Holy Spirit not many days hence." In Acts 2:4, when this promise was fulfilled, we read, "They were all filled with the Holy Spirit." In Acts 1:4 the same experience is spoken of as "the promise of the Father," and in Luke 24:49 as "the promise of my

Father" and "endued with power from on high." By comparing Acts 10:44, 45, and 47 with Acts 11:15, 16, we see that the expressions "the Holy Ghost fell on them" and "the gift of the Holy Ghost" and "received the Holy Ghost" are all equivalent to "baptized with the Holy Ghost" (13-14). Notice that the King James Version of the Holy Bible, published in 1611, uses the term "Ghost" while the New International Version and most modern language versions use the term "Spirit." The two terms are used interchangeably.

Don Basham, in *A Handbook on Holy Spirit Baptism*, says that the Greek term for baptism can mean "identification with" and "overwhelming"; therefore, when Jesus said, "you will be baptized with the Holy Spirit" (Acts 1:5), Basham likes to translate it this way: "You will be flooded with the Holy Spirit" (65). Certainly, Basham agrees with G. Raymond Carlson that it is quite clear that the 120 on the Day of Pentecost received an overwhelming experience in God (24); they were completely immersed—spirit, soul, and body—in the Holy Spirit. In like manner, Frank B. Rice points out that a baptism is "an overwhelming experience. The Greek equivalent may be translated 'to make whelmed'" (8). The experience had a life-changing impact on those who received. The Holy Spirit entered their lives to change them. In the same way, He enters our lives to change us, to empower us for God's service, to help us bring honor to Christ Jesus and to be our constant companion—both Counselor and Comforter.

The Baptism with the Holy Spirit is not regeneration. The Scripture in I Cor. 12:13, "For by one Spirit are we all baptized into one body" refers to the act of the Holy Spirit placing believers into the body of Christ—into salvation. The Holy Spirit is the agent who places believers in Christ. However, Christ is the Agent who baptizes believers with the Holy Spirit (see Matt. 3:11, John 1:33, Acts 2:33, Luke 24:49). This experience of the baptism with the Holy Spirit is called the "promise of the Father." Peter's sermon at Pentecost gives evidence of two separate events: (1) "repent and be baptized. . ." and (2) "you will receive the gift of the Holy Spirit" (Acts 2:38).

The Baptism with the Holy Spirit is a second encounter with God—the first is conversion. In the second encounter Christians begin to receive the supernatural power of the Holy Spirit into their lives. This second experience of power is given to Christians to equip them for service and for furthering God's kingdom and ministry. In this spiritual baptism Jesus begins exercising His sovereign possession, control and use of believers through the work of the Holy Spirit (Jorstad, 59). In this baptism the Christian is brought into deeper relationship with Jesus Christ and also with the Holy Spirit and given power so that the Christian can then be an instrument for God's work.

The word "power" associated with the coming of the Holy Spirit, both on the Day of Pentecost and for all who have received the Baptism with the Holy Spirit since then, has two meanings in the English, points out G. Raymond Carlson, in his article "This is That." One means "authority"; the other means "ability." The second meaning, ability, has the meaning of supernatural ability and strength (23). Carlson states that the word means there is "divine equipment, divine energy—nothing less than God Himself in the person of the Holy Spirit coming upon the believer to enable him to witness effectively of Christ" (23).

Baptism with the Holy Spirit is not water baptism. Water baptism is a public declaration of a changed life resulting from conversion. In fact, there are several specific baptisms for all believers. When people are converted, they are baptized into Christ. After conversion, believers are commanded to be baptized in water. Then the next step is Baptism with the Holy Spirit.

The first event in a new believer's experience is baptism into the body of Christ—salvation, also called regeneration. At the time a sinner repents of sin and accepts Jesus as Savior, he is baptized by the Spirit into the body of Christ—the Church. The Holy Spirit is the baptizer. This starts the sinner on a new way of life—a life of regeneration. The Church, then, has the duty to baptize this new believer in water as a means of recognition that there has been a change from sin to redemption—a new way of life. The Church is the agent of this second baptism. The Christian has now been accepted into the Church. Now comes the third step. This regenerated sinner, now a member of Christ's church, must be baptized in the Holy Spirit by the Lord Jesus Christ, the head of the Church. Christ is the agent in this baptism where the believer is baptized into the life of the Holy Spirit.

According to John Stott there is more involved in a baptism than is apparent. For example, Stott says there are four parts in every kind of baptism—including baptisms in water, blood, Spirit, fire. The four parts are the subject (the baptizer), the object (the baptized), the element with or in which one is baptized, and the purpose for the baptism. For example, the apostle Paul describes the crossing of the Red Sea as a baptism (I Cor. 10:1, 2). God himself was the baptizer. The escaping Israelites were the baptized. The baptism was administered in water, and its purpose was to baptize the people into a relationship to Moses as their God-appointed leader. In John's baptism, John the Baptist was the subject (the baptizer), the people of the region were the objects (the baptized), the baptism took place in the waters of the Jordan River, and the purpose was for repentance (Mt. 3:11). Christian baptism is similar. The minister baptizes the believer with water, into the one name of the Trinity (Matt. 28:19), or into the name of the Lord Jesus Christ (Acts. 8:16, 19:5). The baptism with the Holy Spirit is no exception to this formula. References to baptism with the Holy Spirit almost all follow the same pattern—Jesus Christ is the baptizer. "We all" (I Cor. 12:13) are the baptized. The Holy Spirit is himself the element with which the baptism takes place (Stott, 24-26).

To help clarify any confusion between water baptism and Baptism with the Holy Spirit, let's compare the elements of baptism in water and Baptism with the Holy Spirit so that we can see the significant differences. Don Basham gives the comparison in list form to make those differences even more obvious (23):

Christian baptism by immersion in water would include the following:

1. The candidate: the penitent believer (Matt. 28:19, Acts 2:38)
2. The baptismal element: water (Acts 8:36-38)
3. The baptizer: man—a preacher, evangelist, deacon (Acts 8:38)
4. The purpose: a witness to conversion and the remission of sins (Acts 2:38; 22:16).
5. The result: salvation and entry into the body of Christ (Mk. 16:16, Gal. 3:27).

Baptism with the Holy Spirit, on the other hand, would differ in each of the five areas:

1. The candidate: the baptized believer (Acts 2:38, 8:14-17)
2. The baptismal element: the Holy Spirit (Mk. 1:8)
3. The baptizer: Jesus Christ (Matt. 3:11, Mk. 1:8)
4. The purpose: to endue the Christian with power (Acts 1:8, Luke 24:49)
5. The result: reception of the Holy Spirit with accompanying gifts and powers (Acts 2:4, 8:14-16; I Cor. 12:4-13).

Being baptized by the Holy Spirit in the body of Christ (at salvation) is not an encounter with the Church but with the Holy Spirit, points out David du Plessis. In the same way, Baptism in water is not an encounter with the water but with the Church, and Baptism with the Holy Spirit is not an encounter with the Spirit but with Christ, the baptizer. "This means total surrender and absolute commitment to Jesus. Without this He cannot baptize you in the Spirit" (71).

Water baptism is not essential to salvation, though water baptism is a command of the Lord. In Mark 16:16 Jesus said, "Whoever believes and is baptized will be saved," and in Acts 2:38 Peter preached, "Repent and be baptized, every one of you, in the name of Jesus Christ so that your sins may be forgiven." The requirement for salvation is a personal relationship with Jesus Christ. Jesus Christ regenerates or provides salvation for people when they invite Him into their lives as Lord and Savior and surrender their hearts completely to Him.

What actually takes place when people are baptized with the Holy Spirit? They may be praying alone or with a group. They may be standing, sitting, kneeling, or prostrate. They may be praying loudly or softly. Their thoughts should be focused on the Baptizer, Jesus, in worship, adoration, and praise. They are very aware of the presence of the Lord Jesus Christ and they find their vocabulary tremendously inadequate to express the praise and love in their hearts for the Person who loved them enough to die for them. The prayer may be in hushed tones, in conversational words, or in an ecstatic, explosive outbreak of joyful exhilaration. Human responses vary greatly, but all will speak with tongues when their own words become inadequate enough that they will give the Holy Spirit control of their tongues. Most will be very aware of the nearness of Jesus as never before and will receive power to serve the Savior as never before. The Baptism with the Holy Spirit is the beginning of greater experiences in God. Those filled with the Holy Spirit become channels through whom the supernatural gifts of the Holy Spirit may be transmitted to help others at moments of greatest need (Durasoff, 4).

The Baptism with the Holy Spirit is not essential to salvation either, but it is a gift from God to all who will receive it. The purpose of the Baptism with the Holy Spirit is clear from many passages in Scripture. However, Jesus states in John 16:14 that "He [the Holy Spirit] shall glorify me." This is an all-inclusive expression—including the transformation of the individual believer (2 Cor. 3:18), the training necessary for believers to develop ability in the service of the Lord, and the power necessary for believers to perform the task which God has called them to accomplish (Carlson, 23).

The baptism of the Holy Spirit is available for all Christians. In the words of R. A. Torrey,

> Nevertheless, the baptism with the Holy Spirit is the birthright of every believer. It was purchased for us by the atoning death of Christ, and when He ascended to the right hand of the Father, He received the promise of the Father and shed Him forth upon the church, and if anyone today has not the baptism with the Holy Spirit as a personal experience, it is because he has not claimed his birthright (*The Person and Work of the Holy Spirit,* p. 177).

And Carlson adds that the baptism with the Holy Spirit was the normal experience of all in the Early Church; all believers are entitled to it still. All believers should expect the promise of the Father, the Baptism with the Holy Spirit (25).

The baptism with the Holy Spirit is a **definite experience** and all Christians may know whether or not they have received it. Jesus told His disciples, “stay in the city . . . until you have been clothed with power from on high” (Luke 24:49). How could they have done this if the experience were not definite enough that they could know when they had received it? Paul’s question to the Ephesians confirms the same point: “Did you receive the Holy Spirit when you believed?” (Acts 19:2). Paul expected them to know whether or not they had received the experience, so it had to have been a definite experience with some physical manifestation. In this case R. A Torrey clarifies that in Acts 19:2 they knew they had not received, but in Acts 19:6 they knew they had received (*Baptism*, pp. 14-15).

The Bible uses no vague or indefinite language such as some of our modern theologians use about the signs of baptism. The Bible is definite about salvation too—a person can answer positively and definitively yes or no to the question, “Are you saved?” The Bible is equally definite about the baptism with the Holy Spirit—a person can answer positively yes or no to the question, “Have you been baptized with the Holy Spirit?” (Torrey, *Baptism*, 15).

The baptism with the Holy Spirit is a work of the Holy Spirit **separate and distinct from salvation.** In Acts 1:5 when Jesus told the disciples “in a few days you will be baptized with the Holy Spirit,” they had already been regenerated but they had not yet been baptized with the Holy Spirit. We know they had already been regenerated, notes R. A. Torrey (*Baptism*, p. 16), because Jesus said to them in John 15:3, “Now you are clean through the word” and in John 13:10, “you are clean, though not every one of you” (excepting Judas). Another confirmation that salvation and baptism with the Holy Spirit are two separate experiences appears in Acts 8:12-16 when Peter and John prayed for the regenerated, that they “might receive the Holy Spirit, because the Holy Spirit had not yet come upon any of them.”

Further, on the Day of Pentecost, after the 120 had received the Holy Spirit in the upper room, 3000 people heard the word and repented, believed, and were baptized with water. John R. W. Stott, in *Baptism and Fullness of the Holy Spirit*, states his belief that although we aren’t specifically told that the 3000 received the gift of the Spirit, yet they must have received because Peter had told them that if they repented, believed, and were baptized, they would receive the Spirit. Therefore, according to Acts 2, two separate companies of people, the 120 and the 3000, received the "baptism" or "gift" of the Holy Spirit (17).

The 3000 may not have experienced the rushing mighty wind, the tongues of flame, or the speaking in other tongues in the same way the 120 did, yet they inherited the same promise and received the same gift (Acts 2:33, 39). The difference between them, Stott says, was that the 120 were regenerated before the Holy Spirit came upon them, while the 3000 were unbelievers and received the gift of the Holy Spirit and salvation simultaneously. It happened immediately when they repented and believed (Stott 17).

It is clear, then, that one may be a believer, regenerated, and yet not have the baptism with the Holy Spirit. The baptism with the Holy Spirit is distinct from regeneration. In fact, Torrey states in his *The Holy Spirit, Who He Is, What He Does*, that "it is as clear as language can possibly make it, that it is one thing to be born again and something further, something additional, to be baptized with the Holy Spirit. It is clear and undeniable, therefore, that one may be a regenerate man and not as yet have received the Baptism with the Holy Spirit" (114, quoted in Riggs, 60). Not every regenerate man has the baptism with the Holy Spirit, though every regenerate man may have this experience. If a person has experienced the regenerating work of the Holy Spirit he is a saved man, but he is not fully fitted for service until he has also received the baptism with the Holy Spirit (Torrey, *Baptism*, 17).

The baptism with the Holy Spirit is **always connected with testimony and service**. The baptism is not for the purpose of cleansing from sin, but for the purpose of empowering for service: note Acts 1:5, 1:8, 2:4, 4:31, 4:33. There is no scripture whatsoever to indicate that the baptism with the Holy Spirit brings about the eradication of the sinful nature or the cleansing from sin. It is for the purpose of empowering for service. Though the baptism with the Holy Spirit is not for regeneration, it is an important part of the power Christians need for the daily overcoming of the sinful nature of man. R. A. Torrey explains that believers can walk daily in the power of the Spirit so that they can be "made free from the law of sin and death" (Rom. 8:2), and through the Spirit, man can "mortify the deeds of the body" (Rom. 8:13). As Christians walk daily in the Spirit, Torrey states, the carnal nature is kept in the position of submission or death. But this daily walk in the Spirit is not the baptism with the Spirit nor is it the eradication of the sinful nature—this overcoming of the sinful nature is not something done once and for all; it is something to be momentarily maintained (*Baptism*, 19) and constantly attended to. "Walk in the Spirit, and you will not fulfill the lust of the flesh" (Gal. 5:16).

There are specific consequences of the baptizing work of the Holy Spirit, points out Charles Ryrie. He cites three of the most significant:

A. The Baptism of the Spirit means a resurrection life for the receiver: "For we were all baptized by one Spirit into one body—whether Jews or Greeks, slave or free—and we were all given the one Spirit to drink" (I Cor. 12:13). The one baptism in Ephesians 4:5 speaks of the need for unity among members of that Body of Christ: ". . . one Lord, one faith, one baptism; one God and Father of all, who is over all and through all and in all." In Galatians 3:27 Paul mentions being baptized into Christ, again associating the believer and receiver with the Body of Christ: "for all of you who were baptized into Christ have been clothed with Christ." The baptizing work of the Spirit links the Body of Christ in unity.

B. The Baptism of the Spirit effects the Union with Christ in His death unto the sin nature. Ryrie explains this result as the "means of actualizing our co-crucifixion with Christ"—for examples, see Col. 2:12: "having been buried with him in baptism and raised with him through your faith in the power of God, who raised him from the dead," and Rom. 6:1-10, especially verse 3: "Or don't you know that all of us who were baptized into Christ Jesus were baptized into his death?" (Ryrie, 79). Being associated by baptism into His death, burial, and resurrection is the basis for the death of believers' sin natures and victory over sin. Water baptism is the outward picturing of what the Spirit does in the heart.

C. The Baptism with the Holy Spirit places us in a position in

> Christ which enables us to receive power, but the Baptism does not guarantee that that power will be experienced or displayed in the believer's life (Ryrie, 79). The Corinthians were baptized but fell short of showing God's power in their lives. They were carnal Christians. The Galatians had been baptized (3:27), but were returning to their weak natures: "But now that you know God—or rather are known by God—how is it that you are turning back to those weak and miserable principles?" (Gal. 4:9). To experience what the baptism accomplishes requires continually being filled with the Spirit (Ryrie 79).

We tend to refer to the Baptism with the Holy Spirit as an experience, says T. E. Gannon in "They Were All Filled." He points out, though, that it is not an experience we pass through. Instead it is a plateau of life we enter into. The memory of the infilling with the Holy Spirit lasts, and the energizing, ever-abiding "enabling fullness of the Spirit should result in an extra dimension of Christian life and attainment" (26).

The Baptism with the Holy Spirit is neither the end goal nor the culmination of the Christian life for a believer. Instead it is a beginning to a fuller and richer spiritual life. The Holy Spirit comes to live with believers as a Companion, Helper, and Source of Strength (John 14:16-18).

CHAPTER III

SPEAKING IN TONGUES

Speaking in tongues, sometimes referred to as praying in tongues (the terms can be used interchangeably), is a form of prayer; in this prayer a Christian yields himself to the Holy Spirit and receives from the Spirit a supernatural language. Speaking in tongues is a way of praying which frees the Spirit within and at the same time opens the believer for the infilling of God Himself.

The supernatural language is a miraculous manifestation of God's power, but it combines both human and divine elements and requires both human and divine initiative. Don Basham, in *A Handbook on Holy Spirit Baptism*, claims that tongue speaking is "truly a co-operation between the Christian and the Holy Spirit" (86). Also, to pray in tongues is a matter of one's will according to 1 Cor. 14:14-15. Here Paul says that when he prays in a tongue, *his* spirit prays, not simply his mind. He indicates that he *wills* to pray and sing with *his* spirit—it is a decision he makes, not something forced on him. Speaking in tongues is a matter of the will as is any other action.

When David du Plessis was asked who spoke the tongues when one is Baptized with the Holy Spirit, did the Holy Spirit or the one receiving, he answered, "Both" (72). "You speak," he says, "as He gives the utterance. You talk to God with words that He gives upon your lips" (72). The principle is the same as in Mark 13:11: "Just say whatever is given you at the time, for it is not you speaking, but the Holy Spirit." This step is an act of faith. Mark also reports that "These signs will accompany those who believe: . . . they will speak in new tongues" (Mark 16:17). As soon as Christians believe His word, His promises, and begin to speak, the Spirit gives the words to say (Du Plessis, 72).

Misunderstanding about what role the speaker has in tongue-speaking has hindered some people from ever receiving the baptism with the Holy Spirit. They assume the person receiving is completely passive and that the Holy Spirit takes an inert or completely still tongue and makes it or forces it to utter speech. In other words, the Holy Spirit does it all and the human being is simply His robot. Actually, though, the person receiving the baptism with the Holy Spirit is very actively participating in the experience of speaking in tongues. Simply, man does the speaking while the Holy Spirit furnishes the words. Acts 2:4 states, "They were all filled with the Holy Spirit and began to speak in other tongues as the Spirit gave them utterance." The last phrase of the verse tells us that the Holy Spirit gave the people the words to say, but it also tells us that the people began to speak on their own (Jorstad, 81). As they spoke, the Spirit filled their mouths with the right words. Dr. Albert Hoy adds that the utterance (words, phrases, sentences) was supplied by the Holy Spirit and the disciples "used no conceptual forethought of their own in the vocalization" ("Public and Private," 11). In the same manner, the Christian who speaks with tongues will realize that he does not know before hand what syllables he will utter, but he will speak "not as he receives a mental impression, but as the Spirit gives him the utterance" (Hoy, 12).

Why Speak with Tongues? It's an important question that most believers ask at some time or another. There are many reasons for speaking in a spiritual language. Primarily, though, the Scriptures encourage it. Jesus said it was one of the signs which were to follow the ministry of Christians: "And these signs will accompany those who believe . . . they will speak with new tongues. . . " (Mark 16:17). Paul encourages Christians to make use of tongues: "Earnestly desire spiritual gifts . . . I want you all to speak in tongues . . . I thank God that I speak in tongues . . . (I Cor. 14:1, 5, 18). Speaking in tongues is one of God's gifts, and Christians need all the gifts God offers.

For those who want more Scriptural evidence of the value of speaking in tongues, Dr. Henry Ness, in his booklet "The Baptism with the Holy Spirit" lists twenty biblical reasons for speaking in tongues (quoted by Basham, 93). Here is Ness's list:

1. Speaking in tongues became uniquely identified with the New Testament Church on the Day of Pentecost (Acts 2:4, I Cor. 12-14).
2. Speaking with tongues was ordained by God for the Church (I Cor. 12:28, 14:21).
3. Speaking with tongues is a fulfillment of prophecy (Isa. 28:11, Joel 2:28, Acts 2:16).
4. Speaking with tongues is a sign OF the believer (John 7:38, 39; Mk. 16:17).
5. Speaking with tongues is a sign TO the unbeliever (I Cor. 14:22).
6. Speaking with tongues is a proof of the resurrection and glorification of Jesus Christ (John 16:7; Acts 2:22, 25, 32, 33).
7. Speaking with tongues is an evidence of the baptism with the Holy Spirit (John 15:26, Acts 2:4, 10:45, 46; 19:6).
8. Speaking with tongues is a means of preaching to men of other languages (Acts 2:6-11).
9. Speaking with tongues is a spiritual gift for self-edification (I Cor. 14:4).
10. Speaking with tongues is a spiritual gift for spiritual edification for the Church (I Cor. 14:5).
11. Speaking with tongues is a spiritual gift for communication with God in private worship (I Cor. 14:2).
12. Speaking with tongues is a means by which the Holy Spirit intercedes through us in prayer (Rom. 8:26, I Cor. 14:14).
13. Speaking with tongues is a spiritual gift for "singing in the Spirit" (Eph. 5:18-19, I Cor. 14:15).
14. The Apostle Paul desired that all would speak with tongues (I Cor. 14:5).
15. The Apostle Paul was thankful for the privilege of speaking in tongues (I Cor. 14:13).
16. Speaking with tongues is one of the gifts of the Spirit (I Cor. 12:10).
17. The Apostle Paul ordered that speaking with tongues

should not be forbidden (I Cor. 14:39).

18. Isaiah prophetically refers to speaking with tongues as a "rest" (Isa. 28:12, I Cor. 14:21).
19. Isaiah prophetically refers to speaking with tongues as a "refreshing" (Isa. 28:12, I Cor. 14:21).
20. Speaking with tongues follows as a confirmation of the Word of God when it is preached (Mk. 16:17, 20).

The supernatural language of tongues is the primary evidence that one has received the Baptism with the Holy Spirit. Edith L. Blumhofer, the project director of the Institute for the Study of American Evangelicalism and Assistant Professor of History at Wheaton College, in her book *Pentecost in My Soul*, affirms that Pentecostals believe that the Baptism with the Holy Spirit is always accompanied by speaking in tongues. During the Holy Spirit renewal at the beginning of the twentieth century, tongues speech became known as the "uniform initial evidence" of the Baptism with the Holy Spirit (17). She points out further, though, that this dogmatic-sounding statement doesn't capture other significant factors associated with and equally important in the outpouring of the Holy Spirit. At the same time that tongues were stressed, so were the following two factors stressed:

1. The process orientation of the Baptism with the Holy Spirit—the process of spiritual growth and transformation. Character changes were essential as the early receivers of the Holy Spirit submitted to the Spirit's control and learned to bear the fruit of the Spirit. The process of spiritual discipline was a "spiritualizing of the personality" of the believer. This was not an instantaneous change; it took time and commitment to conform the human personality to God's likeness.
2. The results which authenticated the Baptism with the Holy Spirit—the Baptism was the beginning, not an end in itself. It initiated the believer into the beginning of a walk with Christ that was to continue until the believer became more and more Christlike in his everyday walk with the Lord. Other immediate results included peace, joy, and rest. Receiving the Baptism with the Holy Spirit was a bit of

> heaven on earth. Also most of those who received found a more intense fascination for Christ and a stronger desire for becoming Christlike (19).

To verify that the language should not be the primary object itself of receiving the Baptism with the Holy Spirit, Blumhofer further reports that those who wanted the Baptism with the Holy Spirit were often told not to pray for tongues but to pray to know and experience Christ. The tongues were the evidence, but they were the side benefit—the side effect of knowing Christ—not the main focus of the experience (20). Tongues were considered the "tell-tale sign" of the experience, not the experience itself. How one lived after the Baptism with the Spirit was the proof of the reality of the experience (24).

As an even more important reason for tongues as evidence of the Baptism with the Holy Spirit, Jorstad points outs that the significance of speaking in an unknown language may be that it shows the "willingness to yield our tongues to God" which in itself "may indicate a more profound surrender than almost any other act" (83). The tongue is our most significant means of communication and the most intimate expression of our own personalities. Until God has control over our tongues, His control over us may be partial. James warns us that "no man can tame the tongue" (James 3:8).

Speaking in tongues also carries responsibility. When most people think of glossalalia or tongue speaking or the language of the Holy Spirit, they have a tendency to ask what the purposes might be for such a supernatural manifestation. The specific biblical purposes for such a language are many. This language is used primarily for praising God, but there are other uses for the supernatural language as well (which will be discussed later). Also, though the primary purpose of speaking in tongues may be for one's own devotional life, there are public or corporate uses for tongues as well.

Harold Horton, in his book *The Gifts of the Spirit*, asks us to consider some of the Scriptural purposes of speaking with tongues. His list, focused on purposes for such spiritual language, is as follows:

1. It is the scriptural evidence of the baptism in the Holy Spirit

(Acts 2:4, 19:6),
2. It is a means for men to speak supernaturally to God (I Cor. 14:2),
3. It is a way for believers to magnify God (Acts 10:46),
4. It is a means for men to edify themselves (I Cor. 14:4),
5. It is a way for our spirits as distinct from our understandings to pray (I Cor. 14:14),
6. It is part of the gift of interpretation of tongues that edifies the church (I Cor. 14:5, 12, 13, 26),
7. It is a sign to them that do not believe (I Cor. 14:22),
8. It is one of the gifts divinely appointed for our profit, as a manifestation of the Spirit (I Cor. 12:7, Acts 2:4) (31).

There are specific implications to praying in the Spirit reports Robert W. Graves in "Praying in Tongues." These implications are that God always listens, that God always understands and that God always answers when believers pray in the Spirit. According to the apostle Paul, states Graves, "when we speak in tongues we do not understand what we are saying (otherwise we could always interpret the utterance), but the Spirit helps us to pray, and it is always according to the will of God (Rom. 8:26, 27). In other words, our glossolalic prayers cannot but be in the will of God. Thus, it would seem we are assured of an answer from God" (15).

Most tongues speaking people are called Pentecostals. The Pentecostals are labeled as such because the initial outburst of tongue-speaking took place about 2000 years ago on a Jewish feast day called the Day of Pentecost. It had been celebrated for centuries by all adult male Jews who were able to be in Jerusalem for the feast day. That year the followers of Jesus were also in Jerusalem—but Jesus had just died, been raised from the dead, and then had reappeared to believers. These believers were now gathered in an upper room to pray. The New Testament account says, "when the Day of Pentecost was fully come, they were all with one accord in one place . . . and they were all filled with the Holy Spirit and began to speak with other tongues as the Spirit gave them utterance: (Acts 2:1, 4). Today, consequently, the word *Pentecost* is more closely associated with the charismatic tongue-speakers than with the ancient Jewish feast day (Durasoff, 8-9).

F. Kramaric agrees that tongues is "*the* sign of the baptism of the Spirit [italics are in the original]. . . All gifts which the Spirit brings and gives had already been given individually before Pentecost, except for speaking in other tongues with interpretation! Thus this was the new sign by which the baptism of the Spirit was known" (Kramaric, F., cited in Hollenweger, 342). Harold Horton adds that "The evidence of water baptism at Jerusalem, Caesarea, Ephesus, was not faith nor love, but wetness! It is the same today. The evidence of baptism in the Holy Spirit at Jerusalem, Caesarea, Ephesus was neither faith nor love, but tongues. So it is today. To be baptized merely 'by faith' or tradition without evidence, is not to be baptized at all—either in water or the Holy Ghost" (Horton, *Baptism*, 13).

CHAPTER IV

THE TESTAMENT PERIODS

Since the Baptism of the Holy Spirit is not found in the Old Testament and is not included in any prophecies regarding the millennium, we must give the experience special treatment. John F. Walvoord, in his book titled *The Holy Spirit*, explains that the experience of the Baptism with the Holy Spirit is considered a specific work of the Holy Spirit for the present age, beginning with Pentecost and ending at the resurrection of the righteous when the Church is translated (138). He further points out that if the church be defined as the saints of this age only, the "work of the Holy Spirit in baptizing all true believers into the body of Christ takes on a new meaning. It becomes the distinguishing mark of the saints of the present age, the secret of the peculiar intimacy and relationship of Christians to the Lord Jesus Christ" (138). It is essential, then, to recognize the baptism of the Holy Spirit as the distinguishing characteristic of the Church, the body of Christ.

The Old Testament Period

Some Christians have assumed that the Holy Spirit first came on the Day of Pentecost in Acts when the early church received the outpouring. However, Wayne E. Ward compares what happened at Pentecost with what happened at Bethlehem (8-9). Jesus did not become the Son of God by being born in Bethlehem; the Son of God was with the Father in Heaven from all eternity. He became flesh and blood through His birth, but He did not come into being.

In the same way, the Holy Spirit came to indwell the body of the church through the outpouring at Pentecost, but He had been with the Father from all eternity. He is first seen hovering over the deep at Creation (Gen. 1:2), but at the Day of Pentecost this eternal part of the trinity found a dwelling place in the body of Christ, the Church. Ward says, "Pentecost was to the Spirit what Bethlehem was to the Son—the place of incarnation or embodiment of the Son and the Spirit for their ministry in the world" (9).

In the Old Testament the Holy Spirit does not have a particular dwelling place but permeates the whole of creation. Psalm 104 shows that the Holy Spirit keeps the created order alive and functioning (Ward, 8). In the New Testament, though, the Holy Spirit dwells specifically in Jesus and Jesus' ministry; then He indwells the Church which continues the ministry of Christ in the world. In His activities in the Old Testament, the Holy Spirit came and went; in the New Testament the Holy Spirit had the redemptive work of Jesus as the basis for His work in the Christian believer (Ward, 9).

The subject of the Holy Spirit is not as prominent in the Old Testament as in the New Testament; however, there are 88 direct references to the Holy Spirit in the Old Testament according to Elder Cumming in *Through the Eternal Spirit* (50, cited in Thomas, 9). The Holy Spirit is mentioned clearly and directly in about half of the 39 books of the Old Testament, though in 16 of the 39 books there is no direct reference (9). Frank M. Boyd, in *The Spirit Works Today*, states that the Holy Spirit is mentioned in the Old Testament one third as often as in the New Testament. Thirteen of these references are in the first five books and fourteen of them are in Isaiah (21).

The Old Testament Day of Pentecost was a Jewish harvest festival that took place when the first harvesting had been finished. The Day of Pentecost was 50 days after the Passover. It was a time of thanksgiving and praise to God for the blessings of the year and of the harvest (Hamill, 1).

The work of the Holy Spirit in the Old Testament was not the same as the work of the Holy Spirit in the New Testament. It is true that the Day of Pentecost in the New Testament marked certain distinctive differences in the operation of the Holy Spirit. However, one should not think that the ministry of the Holy Spirit was rare or sparse in Old Testament times. Charles Caldwell Ryrie, in his *The Holy Spirit*, states, "When we speak of the Spirit 'coming' at Pentecost we do not mean that He was absent from the earth before then. He took up His residence in believers at Pentecost although He was present always before" (41). Orchard agrees that the Holy Spirit had been connected with the affairs of men since the very beginning of the planet (5). For example, the Holy Spirit brooded over the waters in Genesis 1:2; He came upon Samson, Gideon, David, and many others to cause them to accomplish marvelous deeds for God (notice especially Hebrews 11).

A. L. Lastinger, in his article "The Holy Spirit in the Old Testament," clarifies the working of the Holy Spirit through Old Testament times. He asserts that the Holy Spirit was certainly known to the Old Testament saints but to different degrees of revelation (13). The revelation of the person of the Holy Spirit is not as complete in the Old Testament as it is in the New Testament, but it is certainly there.

Some believe that the Holy Spirit is simply another name for God and, therefore, He is the same as God the Father. In fact, however, the scriptures in the Old Testament clearly show that God the Father and the Holy Spirit were not the same person. Genesis 1:2, 6:3, Nehemiah 9:20, Psalms 51:11, 104:30, 139:7, Zechariah 4:6, Haggai 2:5, Isaiah 63:10 all witness this distinction showing that the Father and Holy Spirit are two distinct persons. For example, Isaiah 48:16 says, "now the Lord God, and His Spirit, has sent me." Another time Isaiah gives personality to the Holy Spirit when he says, "But they rebelled, and vexed his Holy Spirit" (Isa. 3:10). In Haggai 2:5 God says, "my Spirit remains among you. Do not fear" obviously separating God the Father and the Holy Spirit as two beings functioning individually (Lastinger, 14).

In the Old Testament days, though believers were regenerate, the Holy Spirit did not come upon all believers but instead came upon only special people for specific ministries at special times. But since Pentecost He will come upon and indwell all believers—a universal blessing (John Stott, 15-16). Rene Pache, in his book *The Person and Work of the Holy Spirit*, also indicates that the work of the Holy Spirit under the Old Covenant was not the same as the work of that same Holy Spirit under the New Covenant (30). He believes that in the Old Testament under the Old Covenant the work of the Holy Spirit was characterized in the following ways.

1. The Spirit was not given to all; God "clothed with His Spirit" those whom He called to special ministry, such as Othniel, Gideon, Jephthah to be judges (Judges 3:10, 6:34, 11:29) or the prophets to write the Bible (I Peter 1:10-11).
2. The Spirit was given temporarily and could be withdrawn. For example, Samson was under the control of the Holy Spirit until the Spirit withdrew from Him (Judges 16:20), and Saul had prophesied under the inspiration of the Holy Spirit, but the Spirit afterwards withdrew from him (I Sam. 10:10, 16:14) (Pache, 30).
3. The Work of the Holy Spirit was not complete. Since Christ had not yet been raised for sinners, the Holy Spirit could not raise men up with Him nor make them members of the Body of Christ because it did not yet exist. The Holy Spirit could not yet baptize them into one body (I Cor. 12:13) as He could later, after Christ came, died, and was resurrected.
4. The Holy Spirit acted upon the whole nation of Israel but had not combined it into one body as He did later on for the New Testament Church (Pache, 33).

However, the sovereignty of the Holy Spirit is very clearly shown in the Old Testament. The Holy Spirit used the servants of God, but also at times He used God's enemies. For example, in the Balaam story we are told that "Balaam lifted up his eyes . . . and the Spirit of God came upon him" (Num. 24:2). The Spirit of God also came upon the messengers of Saul who were sent to kill David, and they prophesied (I Sam. 19:20-23).

The functions of the Holy Spirit in the Old Testament are varied. First of all, the Holy Spirit is associated

- with Creation: Gen. 1:2 ("the Spirit of God was hovering over the waters"),
- with human life as a whole: Gen. 6:3 ("My [the Lord's] Spirit will not always contend with man") and Job 33:4 ("The Spirit

of God has made me"),
- with intellectual and artistic capacity: Exod. 35:30-31 ("he has filled him with the Spirit of God, with skill, ability and knowledge in all kinds of crafts"), and
- with man's intellectual and executive ability: Deut. 34:9 ("Now Joshua . . . was filled with the Spirit of wisdom").

In the prophetic books, the Spirit is the author of Divine revelation and inspiration (Isa. 61:1, Ezek 2:2, Micah 3:8 (Thomas, 12). Throughout the Old Testament the Holy Spirit is the vehicle for the Divine revelation and the Agent of the Divine will. In fact, "God is regarded as at work, and, as in the New Testament, the Spirit is 'the executive of the Godhead'" (Thomas, 16).

According to Lastinger, the Holy Spirit serves four basic functions in the Old Testament (14-15):

1. He is a participant in the creation process: "The Spirit of God moved upon the face of the waters" (Gen. 1:2). Job 26:13, Psa. 104:30, 139:7, Job 33:4, Isa. 59:19 all refer to the Holy Spirit's involvement in Creation.
2. He is involved in the regeneration process of God's people: "I will give them an undivided heart and put a new Spirit in them; I will remove from them their heart of stone and give them a heart of flesh" (Ezekiel 11:19). And note the involvement here: "Then the Lord said, 'My Spirit will not contend with man forever'" (Gen. 6:3).
3. He is a teacher and a guide: "Teach me to do thy will; for thou art my God: thy Spirit is good; lead me into the land of uprightness" (Psa. 143:10). Several Old Testament prophets perceive the Holy Spirit as a guide to the believer (see Micah 2:7, Ezekiel 37:14, Haggai 2:5). And in Nehemiah 9:20, when the Priest was speaking to God, he said, "You gave your Good Spirit to instruct them."
4. He equips God's chosen leaders for special purposes for which God had called them. The Spirit of God equipped Joseph for interpreting Pharaoh's dream (Gen. 41:38). Moses had power to judge Israel only through the Spirit of God which gave him that power (Numbers 11:17). Being

> filled with the Spirit of God gave Bezaleel supernatural skill in constructing the Tabernacle (Exodus 31:3, 35:31). The seventy elders of Israel prophesied because the Spirit of God came to rest on them (Numbers 11:25). Joshua was filled with the Spirit when Moses laid hands on him as Moses' successor (Num. 27:18). Both Gideon and Samson, in the book of Judges, were empowered by the Holy Spirit for special tasks God chose for them to perform. Elisha asked for and received a double portion of that same Spirit (2 Kings 2:9, 16) which Elijah had had. The Spirit is said to be in Joshua, and this was God's reason for choosing him to be leader of the people (Num. 27:18). The Spirit was clearly in Daniel (Dan. 4:8, 5:11-14, 6:3). The Spirit also came upon many others and used them in unique relationships and for specific purposes: for examples, see Judges 3:10, 6:34, 11:29, 13:25, I Sam. 10:9-10, 16:13.

The **Nature of the work of the Holy Spirit in the Old Testament** shows in several ways. Charles Ryrie points out that we especially see the Spirit operating in the lives of Old Testament believers in these three ways: A. selective indwelling, B. restraining from sin, and C. enabling for service (41).

A. Selective Indwelling means that the Holy Spirit was not universally experienced by all of God's people at all times. For example, in the Old Testament the Holy Spirit temporarily came upon individuals at certain times to give them supernatural strength, courage, wisdom, revelations, and visions to bring forth His will. He came upon specific individuals such as military leaders (Judges 14:6, 34) and kings and prophets (Genesis 41:38; 2 Samuel 23:2). The Holy Spirit was the prophetic hope of Israel, realized in the New Testament church, to usher in the Messiah and to usher in the last days as signaled by being outpoured upon all God's people, rather than on specific individuals.

Charles Ryrie mentions that there may be no difference between the Spirit being in someone and the Spirit coming upon someone, except that "coming upon" seems to enforce the temporary character of the Spirit's relationship to the people during the Old Testament times (42). The temporary aspect of the Holy Spirit's power was a natural result and a necessary part of the Holy Spirit using someone for a specific ministry or purpose.

Finally, the Holy Spirit filled some believers in the Old Testament, specifically Bezaleel in relation to his leadership of the craftsmen working on the tabernacle (Exodus 31:3, 35:31). This special filling for service presupposed the Spirit's indwelling, or His coming upon them (Ryrie, 42), enabling a person to accomplish a specific task.

Although the Spirit did indwell people in Old Testament times, the Holy Spirit was selective in regards to whom He indwelt and for how long He filled them or came upon them. In John 14:17 Jesus explained to His disciples the Holy Spirit's activity in the Old Testament, when He explained that up to that time the Spirit had been abiding with the people, but after the Day of Pentecost the Spirit would be in them. Ryrie explains that two conclusions can be drawn from Jesus' statement. First, the ministry of the Holy Spirit in the Old Testament was not erratic though it may have been limited to certain persons and to certain times (42). And second, the ministry of the Holy Spirit was different in nature to what it was after Pentecost. The Lord Jesus characterized the ministry as "being with" contrasted to "being in"—a definite difference in ministry type.

B. Restraint of Sin. The Holy Spirit was active in restraining men from sin even from the dawn of human history; for example in Gen. 6:3 God acknowledges that "My Spirit will not contend with man forever." The very names and titles of the Holy Spirit probably had a restraining effect on men as they considered Him, His ministry, and His power. Consider Neh. 9:20 where the Levites declare about God, "You gave your good Spirit to instruct them," and also Psa. 51:10 where David requests God to "Create in me a pure heart, O God, and renew a steadfast spirit within me."

C. Enablement for Service. Special, specific tasks were empowered by the Holy Spirit. Bezaleel, in his enduement for service in the construction of the tabernacle (Exod. 31:3), for example, was given supernatural ability not to the exclusion of his native ability but in addition to it (Ryrie, 43). Some of the judges of the people of Israel were given Spirit enablement (Judges 3:10, 6:34,

11:29). Samson's strength was produced by the Holy Spirit coming upon him (Judges 14:6). David, when he was anointed king by Samuel, was given special enablement: "from that day on the Spirit of the Lord came upon David in power" (I Sam. 16:13).

Limitations of the Holy Spirit's Work:

Just as the Nature of the Holy Spirit's work was specific, so was the work of the Holy Spirit limited. The work of the Holy Spirit was **limited in extent**—not all people enjoyed the enabling of the Spirit. The fact that the new covenant promised for Israel a ministry of the Spirit in a greater way than they had known is proof that the Old Testament work of the Holy Spirit was limited (Isa. 59:21, Ezek. 39:29). The work of the Holy Spirit was also **limited in duration**—the Holy Spirit could be withdrawn from men at any time. Samson was enabled for a time (Judges 13:25) until God withdrew the Spirit (Judges 16:20). Saul was filled with the Spirit (I Sam. 10:10) though the Spirit later withdrew (I Sam. 16:14). David pled with God not to withdraw from him after David had committed his great sin (Psa. 51:11). Finally, the work of the Holy Spirit in the Old Testament was **limited in its effect**—the ministry was not to all individual Israelites. Israel as a nation benefited from the work of the Spirit, because it was a general ministry to the nation as a whole (Neh. 9:20, Isa. 63:10-11, 14) (Ryrie, 43-44).

Preparatory Nature of the Holy Spirit in the Old Testament:

The ministry of the Holy Spirit in the Old Testament was always looking forward, and specifically looking forward with the deliberate intention of preparing men for what was to come. John A. Schep points out that in the Old Testament the greater number of the followers of God were spiritually immature. They had to be guided by the few who experienced the Holy Spirit in or on them. The ceremonial, symbolic temple-worship provided only a very weak picture of the reality to come in the faraway future with Christ's death on the cross (33). The people were not strong enough to stand alone in a heathen world, so God sent the Holy Spirit to give them strength, to give them examples of His power, and to show His love for them as well as His desire to help them.

Isaiah prophesied the coming of Jesus the Messiah: "Here is my servant, whom I uphold, my chosen one in whom I delight; I will put my Spirit on him and he will bring justice to the nations" (Isaiah 42:1-2). This prophecy brought hope to Israel: the Messiah was coming with the Holy Spirit of God on Him. Israel's hope is evident in Isaiah and Joel. Isaiah 44:3 says, "For I will pour water on the thirsty land, and streams on the dry ground; I will pour out my Spirit on your offspring, and my blessing on your descendants." The Holy Spirit would be poured liberally into people's lives. In fact, the time would come when the Holy Spirit would flood the lives of God's people, giving them spiritual power.

Additionally, the prophet Joel prophesied that "afterward, 1 will pour out my Spirit on all people. Your sons and daughters will prophesy, your old men will dream dreams, your young men will see visions. Even on my servants, both men and women, I will pour out my Spirit in those days" (Joel 2:28-29). The "all" means that everyone who calls upon the name of the Lord would be saved and would be able to receive His Spirit.

The main ministry of the Holy Spirit in the Old Testament was in the work of the prophets. Prophetic messages were a divine initiative to bring about divine control of man's life, both individual and collective. The prophets were called of God, received their messages from God, spoke in the name of God, and denounced those who came speaking in their own words instead of God's words (Conner, 26). Clearly a man was a prophet because God put His Spirit in the man—a man was never a prophet first before having the Spirit of God put into Him. Many prophets were temporary, given messages for a specific occasion. Other prophets, though, seem to have had a permanent calling: especially men like Samuel, Elijah, Isaiah, Jeremiah (Conner, 27). These men were not simply message-givers; they were "forthtellers" for God. They were led by the Holy Spirit to speak and interpret God's will for their day and for God's people.

One part of the Holy Spirit's work in the Old Testament, especially among the prophets, was to foretell the coming of the Messiah. Isaiah 11:2, for example, tells of a shoot from Jesse who is to come and bear fruit: "The Spirit of the Lord will rest on him—

the Spirit of wisdom and of understanding." Consequently, the Messiah will have all the qualities necessary to rule. Conner comments that "This Spirit of Jehovah on him is to be a spirit of wisdom and understanding, of counsel and might, of knowledge, and of the fear of Jehovah. He is to judge and rule with patience, grace and righteousness" (Conner, 29)—an amazing work of the Holy Spirit in the life of the Messiah.

We also have the promise of a future age when the Spirit will be with and in all of God's people. Jeremiah 31:31-34 gives the promise of the Lord making a new covenant with his people. He will no longer write his law on stone tablets but in the hearts and minds of His people. Joel 2 tells of the day when the Spirit will be poured out on all people. Joel's language indicates that the Spirit will be available to all of God's people (Conner, 33).

The Old Testament teaching on the Holy Spirit, according to Thomas, could be summarized something like this: "The Spirit is a Divine agent and energy rather than a distinct personality. God is regarded as at work, and, the same way as in the New Testament, the Spirit is 'the executive of the Godhead'" (16). The Spirit is always a Person in activity, says Thomas, not simply an influence. Beecher, in *The Prophets and the Promise*, states that "this Spirit that inspires the prophets is presented to us as a unique being, having personal characteristics, . . . at once identical with and different from Yahweh" (114, 115, qtd. Thomas, 16).

Thomas points out that the Holy Spirit is mentioned in Genesis 1:2 in quite a familiar way, just as He is in the first chapter of Matthew (10), rather than as some stranger who needs to be introduced. The New Testament identifies and connects the Holy Spirit of the New Testament with the Spirit of the Old Testament—showing that there is no fundamental difference between them. In fact the New Testament conception of the Holy Spirit is based on the Old Testament and is intelligible only when considered with the Old Testament view of Him. Thus there is no real explanation in the New Testament of the Holy Spirit; it is assumed that we will know who He is. As a matter of fact, Luke 4, then, is identified with Isaiah 61, and Acts 2 with Joel 2 (10). In both testaments God is at work by His Spirit.

Walter Conner, in his work *The Work of the Holy Spirit: A Treatment of the Biblical Doctrine of the Divine Spirit,* clarifies that usually the God of the Old Testament is seen as transcendent, but the Spirit brings him down to the realm of creation and makes him real (22). The Old Testament represents the Spirit as operative in nature and also in giving extraordinary powers to man. We see that the Spirit of God moved or brooded over chaos where darkness covered the deep (Gen. 1:1). Thus the Spirit was the power to bring order out of chaos and light out of darkness. Later on we see that the Holy Spirit was given for the sake of advancing God's control and direction of Israel as God's chosen people. The recipients, Israel, did not earn or deserve this gift of the Holy Spirit, but He was given for God's purposes, not for the purposes of private individuals (Conner, 24) or even for the purposes of Israel as a whole. For example, Samson received extraordinary physical strength (Judges 14:6). Gideon was used by the Spirit of God to lead Israel to victory (Judges 6:34). These men were direct representatives of Israel as God's chosen people. They received visitations of the Holy Spirit so that they could help bring about God's purposes for Israel.

Clearly, the fullest revelation of the Holy Spirit remained to be given in the New Testament. However, Joel acknowledged this fact when he said, "It shall come to pass *afterward,* that I will pour out my Spirit upon all flesh" (Joel 2:28, italics added). Many Old Testament writers seem to have realized the ministry of the Holy Spirit was to be enlarged at a later date (Lastinger, 15).

The Intertestamental Period

How much specific movement of the Holy Spirit took place during the centuries between Malachi and Matthew is uncertain. Prophecy had given place first to the priesthood, and second to the work of the Scribes whose duty was the exposition of the Law (Thomas, 18). Dr. Swete, in his article "Holy Spirit" published in the Hastings' *Bible Dictionary,* states that "references to the Divine Spirit are rare . . . When prophecy ceased, it seemed as if the presence of the Divine Spirit had been suspended or withdrawn" (404). Swete does add, though, that "The old consciousness of the perpetual activity of the Spirit of God survived" (404) so that we are assured that the Holy Spirit was a part of those 400 years.

Though the Holy Spirit was obviously part of this span of years and undoubtedly active to some extent, however, most scholars tend to agree with A. L. Humphries who states, in his book *The Holy Spirit in Faith and Experience*, that concerning the 400 years between the Testaments "So far as the doctrine of the Holy Spirit is concerned, there was practically no advance made. One thing which strikes us . . . is the paucity of references to the Spirit. And the few which we find seem to be echoes rather than new and living voices" (96). The Holy Spirit was manifested in the distant past through prophets such as Elijah and Isaiah, but there is no written record verifying that any current prophetic activity existed between the Old and New Testaments.

W. H. Griffith Thomas points out that the Holy Scriptures reveal the plan of God specifically and only through the Bible. From the Bible we learn that between Creation and the Coming of Christ, God the Father is preeminent. From the Coming of Christ to the Day of Pentecost, God the Son is prominent. From Pentecost to the present day is the dispensation of the Holy Spirit, with individuals and the Church coming under the guidance of the Holy Spirit (281-282). The work of the Holy Spirit, then, appears to be a biblical work, derived from the Word of God only. Therefore, we should expect no record of any overt work from the Holy Spirit during the time between the Testaments. In fact, Welldon, in *The Revelation of the Holy Spirit,* states that the "Holy Spirit's nature or operation makes no important progress in Apocryphal literature [literature of the intertestamental period]. It remains where it was; . . . it flows underground for two or three centuries until it re-emerges in the fullness of our Lord's own teaching" (51, cited in Thomas, 22). Conner adds that a new day was coming for the people of God. The prophetic voice had been silent in Israel for a long period of time. But that voice is about to be heard again (38).

The New Testament Period

The Day of Pentecost in the Old Testament commemorated the events of Sinai. When God encountered His people at Sinai, God entered into a different kind of relationship with an entire nation. On the Day of Pentecost in the New Testament, God entered into a new relationship not only with individuals but with the collective body, the Church, by pouring out His Holy Spirit on the people assembled. At Sinai, points out James E. Hamill, in "The Pentecostal Experience," God spoke in a way He had never before spoken to a group of people—in an audible voice (1); at Pentecost, God also spoke in a new way both to man and through man. At Sinai there were supernatural sounds such as wind and fire; on the Day of Pentecost in Acts, there were also sounds of rushing winds and the tongues of fire. On both occasions, Sinai and Pentecost, the wind and fire were simply signs calling attention to the significance of the event (1)—that God was entering a new relationship with people.

Pentecost was one of the big celebrations—Israelites came to Jerusalem to worship God. Dr. J. D. Jones used to say, "There are two things vital to the very existence of the Church—Easter and Pentecost. Easter gave the Church its gospel. Pentecost gave it its power" (cited in Hamill, 2). Hamill adds, "Easter is Christ risen in behalf of His Church. Pentecost is Christ released within the heart of His Church" (2). However, clearly, Pentecost is more than just a special day of observance.

The Day of Pentecost brought a climactic change in the plan and purpose of the Church of God. A new dispensation was born—the dispensation of grace, often called the dispensation of the Holy Spirit. Pentecost came to form a church. This Church was to consist of all the redeemed whether Jew or Gentile, slave or rich (Hamill, 2). The observance of a day, the beginning of a dispensation, the marking of the birth of the Church—Pentecost is a glorious experience for the believer. Augustine declared, "The Holy Ghost on this day—Pentecost—descended into the temple of His apostles, . . . appearing no more as a transient visitor, but as a perpetual comforter and as an eternal inhabitant" (Orchard, 7).

We are now living in the dispensation of the Holy Spirit (Thomas, 70). Everything else was preparatory to this; in fact the previous two dispensations were to prepare for the gift of the Holy Spirit which would bring men into fellowship with God and restore the relationship of God and man (70). "The dispensation of the Spirit, . . . did not dawn until the period of preparation was over and the day of out-pouring had come. . . . It is not that His work is more real in the new dispensation than in the old. It is that it is directed to a different end . . . for the perfecting of the fruitage and the gathering of the harvest" (Warfield, cited in Thomas, 70-71).

The baptism with the Holy Spirit is important to dispensationalism, and John Walvoord states that theologians generally have failed to realize the importance of the baptism with the Holy Spirit. There are many causes for this failure. "The distinctive purpose of God for the church is often not given its proper place. The contrasting spheres of law, grace, and kingdom are often confused. The work of the Holy Spirit in baptism, if properly understood, would do much to correct these errors . . . . By the act of the baptism with the Holy Spirit, the present age began at Pentecost. By an act of the Holy Spirit some future day . . . Christ will come to receive [the church] to Himself" (143).

When Simon Peter stood up to preach on that memorable Day of Pentecost in the book of Acts, he explained to the crowd that this day was a fulfillment of the prophecy of Joel 2:28—that God would pour out His Spirit on all people. Peter preached salvation, resurrection, and the Holy Spirit. But he emphasized that this experience was for everyone—to those listening, to their children, and to all that are far off (Acts 2:38-39). We must realize the significance of those words Peter used. He was saying, "This is for you. This is a new day. This is a new dispensation. This is a new glorious hour when God is pouring out His Spirit upon individuals" (Hamill, 2).

Up until Pentecost the Holy Spirit ministered through some believers who were called for a special task and service in some specific capacity. He anointed outstanding people who had been selected for a certain time of service to God. This anointing was usually reserved for prophets, priests, kings, or others of high rank.

But now the 120 (none of whom were prophets or priests or kings) received the fullness of the Holy Spirit. Simon Peter assured them that this supernatural Pentecostal experience was not only for those who had been with Jesus during His ministry on earth, but it was for as many as the Lord would call—everyone. Peter also preached that the Holy Spirit would now be working through individuals, not through the corporate body of believers only. This was a new day—a day when individuals would be able to have the fullness of the Holy Spirit.

The New Testament era began with the outpouring of the Holy Spirit on the Day of Pentecost. This era is also known as the Church age, the era of the Holy Spirit, the era of the Spirit of prophecy, the age of the Spirit of grace, or the era of freedom in Christ. Cardinal Henry Edward Manning, about a century ago in his book *The Temporal Mission of the Holy Ghost*, said this about the ministry of the Holy Spirit: "It is evident that the present dispensation under which we are is the dispensation of the Spirit, or of the Third Person of the Holy Trinity. . . . We are therefore under the personal guidance of the Third Person, as truly as the apostles were under the guidance of the Second" (qtd. Orchard, 5).

At the feast of Tabernacles which took place in the seventh chapter of John, John indicated that "the Holy Spirit was not yet given." How can this statement be reconciled with the references to the ministry of the Holy Spirit in the Old Testament? Orchard explains that just as Jesus existed before the cradle at Bethlehem, so did the Holy Spirit exist before Pentecost as a working member of the Triune God. On the Day of Pentecost, however, "He entered the world in the official capacity as mediator between men and Christ. Therefore, in that sense Augustine is correct when he speaks of Pentecost as the 'birthday of the Spirit'" (7).

Stott explains that what happened on the Day of Pentecost was that first the 120 and then the 3000 were baptized with the Spirit. The result of this baptism with the Spirit was Acts 2:4; "they were all filled with the Holy Spirit." The fullness of the Spirit, then, was the "consequence of the baptism with the Spirit. The baptism was a unique initiatory experience; the fullness was intended to be the continuing, the permanent result, the norm"; for example it is no surprise, but expected, that, "He [Barnabas] was . . . full of the Holy Spirit and faith" (Acts 11:24; see also Acts 6:3, 7:55, 13:52, Luke 1:15, 41, 67) (36, 37).

The baptism with the Holy Spirit given to the 120 on the Day of Pentecost was a unique, unrepeatable event in the history of Redemption (Schep, 33). It marked the end of the Old and the beginning of the New Dispensation. John A. Schep explains it thus:

> With the outpouring of the Holy Spirit at Pentecost . . . Christ had finished His atoning work and fulfilled all that was symbolized by the shadowy temple worship. Now—and for this purpose the Holy Spirit was poured out—the foreshadowed reality could be revealed and experienced (33).

Hebrews chapters 8 through 10 tell us that the earthly high priests of the Old Dispensation are no longer needed. Christ, the true High Priest, had offered Himself as the perfect sacrifice; hence sacrificial worship was no longer necessary. The Holy Spirit now dwells in the hearts of His children—believers constitute a spiritual temple, built of living stones (Schep, 34). Though the Holy Spirit is omnipresent, in a special sense His residence is now on earth. The New Testament Church is the home of the Spirit. The Holy Spirit lives among us, for we have become "the temple of God, and . . . the Spirit of God dwells in us" (I Cor. 3:16).

Pentecost brought the last era of the history of Redemption. The baptism with the Holy Spirit experienced by the 120 at Pentecost marked the beginning of this new and last Dispensation. "Therefore," says Schep, "it was indeed a most significant and unique turning point in the history of Redemption. And as such it did not need any repetition, nor could it be repeated. For according to Jesus' promise, the Holy Spirit had come to abide with the Church forever" (34). Since Pentecost, from the moment the 120 were baptized, the Spirit's work has centered in the Church on earth. The New Testament Church is a Spirit-Baptized, Spirit-filled Church (Schep, 35).

The uniqueness of the baptism with the Holy Spirit of the 120 at Pentecost is also evident from the fact that it was accompanied by signs that have not been repeated. The sound of the rush of a mighty wind and the tongues of fire on the heads of the disciples were significant because the wind and fire had been signs that announced the coming of the Lord. Additionally, Jesus had likened the Spirit to the wind; one can hear the sound of it without knowing where it comes from or where it is going: "The wind blows wherever it pleases. You hear its sound, but you cannot tell where it comes from or where it is going. So it is with everyone born of the Spirit" (John 3:8). Jesus also spoke of a baptism with the Spirit and with fire (Matt. 3:11, Luke 3:16), indicating that the Spirit would purify God's people by consuming their sins. The miraculous, unusual signs let the disciples know that God the Holy Spirit, for Whom they had been praying, was now coming (Schep, 35).

Later, when others received the baptism with the Holy Spirit, those previous signs were not part of the experience. There was usually one sign: the speaking with other tongues. Schep believes that the fact that the 120 spoke in existing languages which they had never learned was probably unique—this miracle was not necessary to make the hearers understand what the 120 said. Peter addressed the crowd in Aramaic and everyone knew that language, so no interpretation was needed. "The speaking in existing foreign languages was probably meant as a sign that from now on the Church would become universal" (35).

According to Walvoord there are eleven specific references to Spirit baptism in the New Testament. He lists the following: Matt. 3:11, Mark 1:8, Luke 3:16, John 1:33, Acts 1:5, Acts 11:16, Rom. 6:1-4, I Cor. 12:13, Gal. 3:27, Eph. 4:5, Col. 2:12. He points out that all references prior to Pentecost are prophetic. All references after Pentecost treat the baptism with the Holy Spirit as an existing reality (139). The gift of tongues in I Cor. 12 and 14 was certainly different from the tongue speaking of the 120 on the Day of Pentecost. In Corinth the gift of tongues consisted in speaking in totally unknown languages, languages which no one could understand, including the speaker, unless the Holy Spirit granted the interpretation. At Pentecost, no Spirit-given interpretation was needed.

Additionally, the 120 were directly baptized with the Holy Spirit, with no introductory ministry of prayer or laying on of hands as we read occurred in other cases of Spirit baptism in Acts. Everything, therefore, "indicates clearly that the baptism with the Holy Spirit of the 120 was something unique and unrepeatable. It marked the beginning of the New Dispensation. The Holy Spirit made His triumphal entry into the Church, never to leave her again" (Schep, 36).

Characteristics of the Baptizing Work in the New Testament:

A. It is limited to this age. The baptizing work of the Holy Spirit is not found in any other dispensation. Theologically this statement is proved based on I Cor. 12:13: "For we were all baptized by one Spirit into one body—whether Jews or Greeks, slave or free—and we were all given one Spirit to drink." If the baptizing work of the Spirit places a person in the body of Christ, and if the Body of Christ is distinctive to this age (because of the resurrection and ascension of Christ), then so is the baptism (Ryrie, 76). Biblically this statement is supported because the baptizing work is never mentioned as being part of the Old Testament experience nor a part of Christ's earthly ministry. After His resurrection and before His ascension, Christ spoke of the work of the Holy Spirit as yet being future: "For John baptized with water, but in a few days you will be baptized with the Holy Spirit" (Acts 1:5). It happened first on the Day of Pentecost (Peter's statement in Acts 11:15-17). The Spirit will undoubtedly be active in the millennial age, but no specific mention of His baptizing work during that time is given in the Bible. Therefore we can conclude that the baptism with the Holy Spirit is a work particular to this age (Ryrie, 76).

B. It is repeated anew for each person who receives the baptism, but the initial experience comes only once to each believer. Some teach that the baptizing work of the Spirit was never repeated after Pentecost. However we see the repetition of giving the gift of tongues in the house of Cornelius (Acts 10:46), in Ephesus (Acts 19) and other places in the New Testament. Nevertheless, each believer is baptized with the Holy Spirit only once. There is no scriptural reference to support a person being baptized a second time. In fact, the aorist tense of I Cor. 12:13 would indicate an unrepeated experience. However, the same group or person may experience a refilling of the Spirit more than once (see Acts 2:4, 4:31), and the command in Eph. 5:18 to be filled with the Spirit is expressed in the present tense:

> "Do not get drunk on wine, which leads to debauchery. Instead, be filled with the Spirit" (Ryrie, 77), or, more accurately, be continually being filled with the Holy Spirit. Such experience will be confirmed by speaking in tongues.

As an initiatory event the baptism is not repeatable. It cannot be lost, either. However, the filling can be repeated and certainly needs to be maintained. If it isn't maintained, the Holy Spirit will not remain in a sinful heart. If the fullness of the Spirit is lost, however, it can be recovered. The Holy Spirit is "grieved" by sin (Eph. 4:30) and ceases to fill those who grieve him by sinning. Repentance is the only way to be filled again. Some people are filled again even though there has been no sin to take them away from the Holy Spirit. A fresh crisis or challenge in life may demand a fresh enduing of power by the Holy Spirit. For example, in Acts 4:8 Peter was filled again with the Holy Spirit, and in Acts 4:31 the whole company of believers was filled again. Ephesians 5:18 commands all Christians to be filled, or as the continuous present imperative tense implies, to go on being filled with the Spirit (Stott, 37). Stott continues, "These references to the fullness of the Spirit, both describing how certain Christians were filled and exhorting others to be filled, show that it is possible, and all too common, for Christians who have been baptized with the Spirit to cease to be filled with the Spirit" (38).

If one were to ask, "what is the general teaching of the New Testament regarding the reception of the Holy Spirit," there is a plain answer. We receive the Holy Spirit "by hearing [the gospel] with faith" (Gal. 3:2), or more simply "through faith" (Gal. 3:14). Consequently, all God's sons

- possess the Spirit (Gal. 4:6),
- are led by the Spirit (Rom. 8:14), and
- are assured by the Spirit of their sonship and of God's love (Rom. 5:5, 8:15, 16).

Those who do not possess the Spirit do not belong to Christ at all (Rom. 8:9, Jude 19) (Stott, 18). However, though all believers have received the Holy Spirit at conversion, not all have received the Baptism with the Holy Spirit, a separate indwelling by the Holy Spirit.

Elder Cumming, in *Through the Eternal Spirit*, points out that the Holy Spirit in the New Testament is associated with the words "giving" on the part of God and "receiving" on the part of men. But there are other expressions as well. Expressions including such as these—"came upon" (Acts 19:6), "anointed with" (Acts 10:38), "poured out" (Acts 10:45), "fell on" (Acts 10:44), "baptized with" (Acts 11:16), "received" (Acts 2:38)—all show that there are many different ways of regarding the same experience of the Holy Spirit filling the believer (p. 157, cited in Thomas 278).

In the New Testament, states Alasdair Heron, the Holy Spirit enters on center stage as "the Spirit of your Father" (Matt. 10:20), "the Spirit of his Son (Gal. 4:6), "the Spirit of Jesus" (Acts 16:7), "the Spirit of Christ" (Rom. 8:9), "The Spirit of life" (Rom. 8:2), "the Spirit of sonship" (Rom. 8:15), "the Spirit of Grace (Heb. 10:29), "the Paraclete" (John 14:16), "the Spirit of truth" (John 14:17), and the Spirit of wisdom (Acts 6:3, 10). The bearer of these titles is inherently involved in Jesus Christ and His resurrection. The primary message the New Testament offers, apart from the Old Testament and the Intertestamental writings is that the Messiah has come. The age of the Spirit has opened. The Spirit itself is the power of the divine purposes of God the Father and Jesus Christ. All that the New Testament has to say about the Holy Spirit points to that center (Heron, 39): Jesus Christ and Him glorified.

CHAPTER V

THE GOSPELS

The Gospels show a transition in the Scriptures, points out Rene Pache, in his book *The Person and Work of the Holy Spirit*. The New Covenant has come to earth with Christ. Christ lays the foundation for the dispensation that will come after His resurrection. The Church did not begin until Pentecost and with the descent of the Holy Spirit. The Gospels, then, present the teachings of Christ about the Holy Spirit and the New Covenant of grace. The work of the Holy Spirit is characteristically the same as it was in the Old Testament, with a few variations. Luke tells us that John the Baptist would be full of the Holy Spirit even from his mother's womb and that Elisabeth and Zacharias were also filled with the Holy Spirit and able to prophesy about the Messiah (Luke 1:15, 41, 67).

These experiences were equivalent to the experiences of the prophets in the Old Testament when the Holy Spirit came upon them for a special purpose. The Nazarites and prophets called of God in the Old Testament were sometimes singled out from the womb as servants of God—for example note Samson and Samuel and Moses. Simeon, in the temple, is another example. We are told that Simeon "was righteous and devout . . . and the Holy Spirit was upon him" (Luke 2:25-27) and that he had been told he would not die before he had seen the Christ.

On the day of Christ's resurrection, however, the disciples had a very different experience. When Jesus appeared to them, He breathed on the disciples and said, "Receive the Holy Spirit" (John

20:22). In breathing on His disciples, Jesus gave them a token of the real gift that they would receive fully on the Day of Pentecost when they entered into the New Covenant, the dispensation of Grace or the dispensation of the Holy Spirit. We know this breathing was not the full experience of the Holy Spirit because Jesus had also told them that the Holy Spirit would not come until Jesus had gone to the Father. Further, forty days later Jesus told them to wait for the promise of the Father (Acts 1:4). Therefore, the disciples were not baptized with the Holy Spirit until the Day of Pentecost, but the Lord Jesus gave them signs and promises to keep them waiting until the time would be ready for them to receive (Pache, 37-39). In fact, just before Jesus ascended, He told the disciples "Do not leave Jerusalem, but wait for the gift my Father promised, . . . in a few days you will be baptized with the Holy Spirit" (Acts 1:4, 5).

The disciples, then, belonged to two dispensations (Pache, 40). They received a measure, a promise, of the Spirit before they received the baptism with the Holy Spirit at Pentecost. They had belonged to the old covenant, but now their faith required them to make a leap into the new covenant by believing Jesus and all that He had promised them.

Henry Barclay Swete, in his article "Holy Spirit" in *Hastings Bible Dictionary*, reports that "The Gospel history opens with an outburst of prophecy. Such a revival of prophetic gifts had not occurred since the days of Ezra and Nehemiah" (405).

The association of the Holy Spirit with the Incarnation is the first manifestation of the Holy Spirit's prophetic ministry in the New Testament. The Angel told Mary that the child in her would be conceived by the Holy Spirit. The Angel spoke to Mary much in the language of the Old Testament, thus connecting Old Testament prophetic methods with a New Testament message. The sinlessness of Christ resulted from the Holy Spirit. Swete comments further that "The ministry of the Baptist was a link between the old order and the new, and when Jesus began to teach, He took up the thread which John had been compelled to drop. In John the Baptist the prophetic Spirit uttered its last testimony to Him that was to come, completing the witness of the Old Testament at the moment when the Christ was ready to enter upon His work" (Swete, *The Holy*

Spirit in the New Testament, 22).

The Holy Spirit in the Gospels is often associated with some specific function or service. For example we see John the Baptist's ministry predicted in Luke 1:15-17: "he will be filled with the Holy Spirit, even from his mother's womb. . . to make ready for the Lord a people prepared." Mary received the Holy Spirit for the function of being the mother of Jesus: "The Holy Spirit will come upon you and the power of the Most High will overshadow you" (Luke 1:35). Elizabeth received the Holy Spirit and prophesied to Mary: "and Elizabeth was filled with the Holy Spirit and she exclaimed with a loud cry, 'Blessed are you among women'" (Luke 1:41-42). Zechariah, the father of John the Baptist, was filled with the Holy Spirit when he was willing to believe and prophesy about his son's ministry. In each case the writer Luke connects being filled with the Holy Spirit to some function, service, office or ministry (Ranaghan, 69).

Also when Jesus comes to the Jordan to be baptized, the Holy Spirit is seen coming upon Him (Luke 3:21-22) and Jesus is spoken of as "full of the Holy Spirit" (Luke 4:1). The Holy Spirit was certainly evident at the baptism of Jesus. In fact some call this experience the consecration of the Messiah. His ministry had not yet been public. The Divine recognition and acceptance by the Father God brought new powers (Thomas, 53) with a new consciousness of God's mission through the Son. Through the guidance of the Holy Spirit Jesus came to the Jordan for baptism and to receive the anointing of the Holy Spirit for the work ahead of Him (Matt. 3:16, John 3:34). Frank M. Boyd, in his book *The Spirit Works Today,* emphasizes that the "dynamic of all of Christ's activities must be attributed to His anointing by the Holy Spirit, rather than to His deity" (31). The anointing Jesus received at the Jordan was more than a temporary giving of spiritual power of His own ministry; it was, according to Boyd, "a sign that He was the One who would impart the Holy Spirit to others" (32).

All four Gospels present the baptism of Jesus as His time of anointing, as the time when the Holy Spirit of God comes upon Him and the voice from heaven decrees that Jesus is God's beloved Son (Matt. 3:16-17; Mark 1:10-11; Luke 3:22; John 1:32-34). "In the power of the Spirit" then, Jesus returned from the desert of temptation after His baptism and began teaching in the synagogues (Luke 4:14-15). While teaching in the Synagogue, Jesus read the passage from Isaiah 61:1: "The Spirit of the Lord is upon Me." Then Jesus pronounced "Today this Scripture is fulfilled in your hearing" (Luke 4:21). Jesus established the pattern of demonstrating power, authority, healing, and preaching effectiveness after He received the manifestation of the Holy Spirit (Bundrick, 16). In the same way, the disciples reacted with those same demonstrations after they had received the outpouring of the Holy Spirit—power, authority, healing, and preaching effectiveness. Humphries, in *The Holy Spirit in Faith and Experience*, states that "from the Baptism the presence of the Holy Spirit in Jesus, instead of being viewed as occasional or fitful, as was sometimes the inspiration of the prophets, was regarded as permanent, and as the power in which all His Messianic duties were discharged" (p. 137, qtd. Thomas 58).

From the time of the Last Supper through the crucifixion, Jesus stresses the work of the Holy Spirit more than ever before. He makes it clear to His disciples that He will be with them no longer but that He will send the Holy Spirit to be with them. The new life of the new Church is definitely linked with the coming of the Holy Spirit (John 14, 15, 16). The Holy Spirit is the key to the new life of faith the disciples and the Church will experience after Jesus returns to the Father.

The principal and primary work of the Holy Spirit throughout the Gospels, though, is His work in the life of Jesus. All four Gospels emphasize the place of the Holy Spirit in the life of Jesus. Every part of Jesus' earthly life is intimately connected with the Spirit (Barclay, *Promise*, 22).

Christ was born of the Holy Spirit: in Matt. 1:20 God made known to Joseph that the child conceived in Mary was of the Holy Spirit. Then when our Lord's ministry was about to begin, we see the Holy Spirit again. John the Baptist tells us that the Holy Spirit descended on Christ in the form of a dove.

Jesus Christ was anointed with the Holy Spirit: John 5:19 tells us that "The Son can do nothing of himself but what he sees the Father doing." Jesus confirms this when He quotes Isaiah: "The Spirit of the Lord is upon me because he has anointed me to preach good tidings . . ." (Luke 4:18). Acts 10:38 reports "God anointed him [Jesus of Nazareth] with the Holy Spirit and with power."

The Holy Spirit lived in Jesus: at Jesus' baptism the Spirit descended and remained on him (John 1:33).

Christ was filled with the Holy Spirit: Jesus returned from his baptism in the Jordan filled with the Holy Spirit (Luke 4:1).

Jesus was also led by the Spirit: during the 40 days of his temptation by the devil, "Jesus was led by the Spirit in the wilderness" (Luke 4:1, 2).

Christ was raised by the Holy Spirit: "If the Spirit of him who raised Jesus from the dead is living in you, he who raised Christ from the dead will also give life to your mortal bodies through his Spirit, who lives in you" (Rom. 8:11).

The work of Jesus in the gospels was to bring God into the lives of men. For this purpose He was anointed of the Spirit of God. Jesus was given over to the Spirit. He possessed the power of God. The Spirit of the Lord was upon him to do the work of God (Conner, 50). As the Old Testament kings were given special wisdom, points out Bundrick, so was Jesus given the spirit of wisdom after His baptism (16). We are told that the crowds were amazed at His wisdom (Mark 6:2, Matt. 13:54), and later Paul confirms that He [Jesus Christ] is "the wisdom of God" (I Cor. 1:24, 30) and that in Him are "hid all the treasures of wisdom and knowledge" (Col. 2:3).

Jesus was described as being full of the Spirit: Luke 4:1, "Jesus, full of the Holy Spirit, returned from the Jordan and was led by the Spirit in the desert." Barclay indicates that when the phrase "full of the Spirit" is used of Jesus, it has a special significance. Before this time, when the prophets of the Old Testament were full of the Holy Spirit, their experience was transitory and spasmodic; the Spirit used them at times only for particular messages. "But for Jesus," says Barclay, "the Spirit was a lasting, permanent, abiding, inalienable equipment. What they had at sundry times and in divers manners, what they had in a measure that was partial and fragmentary and impermanent, He had for ever" (*Promise*, 23). The Spirit guided Jesus and directed His life and actions, and it was the Holy Spirit who empowered Jesus for His ministry.

The Holy Spirit equipped Jesus for His ministry in the world: the prophetic word from Isaiah was fulfilled in Jesus (Isa. 42:1). The miracles performed by the Son of God are often associated with the Holy Spirit—especially with the power of the Holy Spirit. In Matt 12:28 Jesus claimed to "drive out demons by the Spirit of God." And in Luke 10:21, the statement about Jesus being "full of joy through the Holy Spirit," indicates that the Holy Spirit was definitely present and powerful in the ministry of Jesus Himself (Thomas, 55).

In His role as the Spirit of Christ, the Holy Spirit functions in the specific role of revealing the essential nature and divine vitality of the Son of God (John 4:14, 7:37-39). John also affirms that the Savior's abiding presence in the regenerated life is realized through the agency of the Holy Spirit: "By this we know that he abides in us, by the Spirit which he has given us" (I John 3:24). In His role as the Spirit of Christ, the Holy Spirit continued prophetic revelations of our Lord up to the time Christ was baptized by John the Baptist. Simeon and Anna both testified that the Child Jesus was the Messiah (Luke 2:25-38) and John the Baptist identified the person on whom the dove descended as the Son of God (John 1:33, 34) (Barclay, *Promise,* 25).

Clearly, then, the Holy Spirit is manifested at each stage of Jesus' life and work: at His Birth, Baptism, Temptation, life, ministry, teachings, and also His death and resurrection (Thomas, 56). Jesus Christ needed the assistance of the Holy Spirit in His birth, His ministry, His death, His resurrection. If Jesus needed the Holy Spirit, how do we dare think we can get along without this wonderful gift our Father has sent to us? We cannot hope to live a Christian life without the presence and fullness of the Holy Spirit to give us power to do it. We receive that power when we receive the Baptism with the Holy Spirit.

Though his article deals mostly with the contrast of the Holy

Spirit to humanism, Amos D. Millard mentions some functions of the Holy Spirit that are pertinent to a look at the Gospels. He points out that the Scripture clearly teaches that the Holy Spirit has specific functions in the Gospels as well as in the New Testament as a whole.

1. The Holy Spirit will bring glory to Christ. In John 15:13, 14 Jesus states "He [the Holy Spirit] will bring glory to me by taking what is mine and making it known to you."
2. The Holy Spirit is concerned about the future. "When he, the Spirit of truth, comes, he will guide you into all truth. . . . He will tell you what is yet to come" (John 16:13).
3. The Holy Spirit is involved in the reconciliation between God and man. "When he comes, he will convict the world of guilt in regard to sin and righteousness and judgment; in regard to sin, because men do not believe in me; in regard to righteousness, because I am going to the Father . . . and in regard to judgment, because the prince of this world now stands condemned" (John 16:8-11).
4. The Holy Spirit cares for men's souls. "He will guide . . . into all truth . . . he shall speak . . . he will show . . . He shall glorify me [Christ]" (John 16:13, 14).

The person and work of the Holy Spirit emphasize the necessity of a supernatural intervention of God for the solution to man's problems (6, 7).

One of the primary functions of the Holy Spirit was the preparation for or in the relation to the Church that was to be established. Jesus' discourses in John 14, 16, and 20 link the life of the Church with the coming of the Holy Spirit. In John 20:20-23, after Jesus had risen from the grave, He greeted His disciples by saying, "'As the Father has sent me, even so I send you.' And when he had said this, he breathed on them, and said to them, 'Receive the Holy Spirit. If you forgive the sins of any, they are forgiven; if you retain the sins of any they are retained.'" This passage shows several things about the Holy Spirit in relation to the Church.

1. The sending of the Holy Spirit came after the resurrection and follows closely Jesus' instruction to Mary to tell the disciples, "I am returning to my Father . . . (John 20:17).

Clearly, then, the sending of the Spirit is an act of the risen, glorified Lord Jesus.

2. Receiving the Holy Spirit is closely connected with the commission or ministry of the disciples to be sent out to the world. By the power of the Holy Spirit the Church continues Jesus' ministry to the world.
3. Receiving the Holy Spirit is connected to the power and function to forgive sin. The reconciliation of man to God and man to man is the purpose of the birth, death, and resurrection of Jesus. That same redeeming ministry is given to the Church.

Therefore, we can see that this passage addresses the functions and ministry of the Church (Ranaghan, 74). The key to the Church's being able to function at all and to continue to exist and grow comes when Jesus bestows the Holy Spirit on the disciples and the Church.

In fact Jesus bestowed the Holy Spirit on the Church on Easter Sunday evening. As Jesus greeted His disciples, showing them His hands and side, He said, "'As the Father has sent me, even so I send you.' And when he had said this, he breathed on them, and said to them, 'Receive the Holy Spirit'" (John 20:20-23). Notice that the coming of the Holy Spirit—Jesus breathing the Holy Spirit on the disciples—is closely associated with the ministry of the disciples to be sent as Jesus had been sent. By the power of the Holy Spirit the new Church would be the continuation in the world of Jesus' ministry (Ranaghan, 74).

Luke shows God sending out His Spirit to work in the lives of men and bring them into harmony with Himself (35). In the first two chapters of his gospel, Luke gives a series of manifestations of the working of the Holy Spirit. For example the Holy Spirit's encounters with Mary, Elizabeth, Zacharias, and Simeon all are specific instances where the Holy Spirit met people to bring about God's purposes and kingdom. These instances are reminiscent of the prophetic inspiration of the Old Testament. These were evidently times when the Holy Spirit came temporarily to fulfill a purpose of God. John the Baptist prophesied that the risen Christ would baptize with the Holy Spirit and power. This promise was fulfilled in Acts. The end of the Gospels, then, and the book of Acts fit into each other in telling about the Spirit as that Spirit was poured out upon his waiting disciples (Conner, 53).

The general idea of the Holy Spirit in the Gospels is that the Holy Spirit is the Divine power at work in and on Christ, promised to the disciples for the founding of the new Church, and the revealer of Christ as the Messiah (Conner, 56).

CHAPTER VI

TONGUES IN ACTS

Jesus gave the Holy Spirit on the Day of Pentecost, 50 days after Passover. According to Acts 1:15, about 120 Jewish people waited in Jerusalem, including the 12 apostles and the disciples. Acts 1:14 lets us know that this number included women. Children were probably there too.

Acts 2:1-4 says, "When the day of Pentecost came, they were all together in one place. Suddenly a sound like the blowing of a violent wind came from heaven and filled the whole house where they were sitting. They saw what seemed to be tongues of fire that separated and came to rest on each of them. All of them were filled with the Holy Spirit and began to speak in other tongues as the Spirit enabled them." One hundred and twenty followers of Jesus Christ prayed in the Spirit. The 120 were not preaching, but they were praying as they had been doing daily, waiting for the Holy Spirit to come. With the outpouring of the Holy Spirit on them, the 120 believers made a move of faith from praying with their intellect to worshiping in the Spirit.

The crowd, hearing the noise, went to see what was going on and what was causing all the commotion. To their surprise, they saw and heard the gospel in their own languages. Luke reports in Acts 2:5-13,

> Now there were staying in Jerusalem God-fearing Jews from every nation under heaven. When they heard this sound, a crowd came together in bewilderment, because each one heard them speaking in his

> own language. Utterly amazed, they asked: 'Are not all these men who are speaking Galileans? Then how is it that each of us hears them in his own native language? Parthians, Medes and Elamites; residents of Mesopotamia, Judea and Cappadocia, Pontius and Asia, Phrygia and Pamphylia, Egypt and the parts of Libya near Cyrene; visitors from Rome (both Jews and converts to Judaism); Cretans and Arabs—we hear them declaring the wonders of God in our own tongues!' Amazed and perplexed, they asked one another, 'What does this mean?' Some, however, made fun of them and said, 'They have had too much wine.'

When so many Jews heard the gospel in their own languages, and were astonished that uneducated Galileans spoke foreign languages, they accused the believers of being drunk. Peter responded to the charge of drunkenness by giving his first Post-Pentecost sermon of power. Acts 2:14-18 tells us what he said:

> Fellow Jews and all of you who are in Jerusalem, let me explain this to you; listen carefully to what I say. These men are not drunk, as you suppose. It's only nine in the morning! No, this is what was spoken by the prophet Joel: 'In the last days, God says, I will pour out my Spirit on all people. Your sons and daughters will prophesy, your young men will see visions, your old men will dream dreams. Even on my servants, both men and women, I will pour out my Spirit in those days, and they will prophesy.'

As Peter continued preaching, telling how Jesus, who had been crucified, had also been resurrected and had ascended into heaven, many Jews then believed. The believing ones asked, "Brothers, what shall we do?" (Acts 2:37). Peter answered in Acts 2:38-39, "Repent and be baptized, every one of you, in the name of Jesus Christ so that your sins may be forgiven. And you will receive the gift of the Holy Spirit. The promise is for you and your children and for all who are far off—for all whom the Lord our God will call."

Three thousand Jews responded to Peter's sermon, were saved, and received the Holy Spirit.

Two significant references to Baptism with the Holy Spirit are found in Acts (1:5, 11:16), and these two passages are complementary.

In Acts 1:5 the author of Acts, Luke, re-states Jesus' last words, "Do not leave Jerusalem, but wait for the gift my Father promised, which you have heard me speak about. For John baptized with water, but in a few days you will be baptized with the Holy Spirit." Notice two important facts in these statements: (1) Up to this time the Holy Spirit had not baptized the disciples, the followers of Christ; (2) they would receive the baptism in or with the Holy Spirit in a few days—"not many days hence" according to the King James Version (Walvoord, 144). They were told to wait in Jerusalem until they were baptized by the Holy Spirit (Acts 1:4). The indications are clear that this prophecy was fulfilled on the Day of Pentecost. And Jesus said in verse 8 of the same chapter, "But you will receive power when the Holy Spirit comes on you; and you will be my witnesses in Jerusalem, and in all Judea and Samaria, and to the ends of the earth."

The second passage (Acts 11:16) confirms Acts 1:5. Peter said, about the conversion of Cornelius and those who were gathered in his house,

> As I began to speak, the Holy Spirit came on them, as he had come on us at the beginning. Then I remembered what the Lord had said, 'John indeed baptized with water, but you will be baptized with the Holy Spirit.' So if God gave them the same gift as he gave also to us, who believed in the Lord Jesus Christ, who was I to think that I could oppose God? (Acts 11:15-17).

Peter is clearly stating that the baptism has been fulfilled already, no doubt a reference to Pentecost. John Walvoord points out that the proof that Cornelius and his household had been baptized by the Holy Spirit is found in the fact that they spoke with tongues (Acts 10:46) (Walvoord, 144). Jesus said that believers would be baptized with the Holy Spirit when they received the Holy Spirit. The manifestations which attended the reception of the Holy Spirit confirmed the baptism with the Holy Spirit. In Scripture, tongues was consistently the initial physical evidence of receiving the Holy Spirit.

The confirmation that Jesus indeed was sending the Holy Spirit comes in Acts chapters 1 and 2. These events again stress that, with the coming of the Holy Spirit whom the disciples are to wait for, the Church and the disciples will receive power—power to witness of Christ and to preach the gospel throughout the world (Ranaghan, 75).

In the record of the events on the Day of Pentecost in Acts 2, we can notice several points.

1. The new church is filled with the Holy Spirit and for the first time the gospel is publicly preached with such power and attraction that a large number of people are converted to Christ and brought into the Church. Clearly the new dynamic power in the Church is the Holy Spirit.
2. The Holy Spirit's coming is accompanied by corporeal (sensible, easily identifiable) phenomena—the sound of the rushing wind, the appearance of fire-like tongues, and the speaking in other than usual languages.
3. Peter assumes leadership and begins his first public preaching. He assures the audience that the group is sober (not drunk)—so we assume a large part of the group could not understand the tongues being spoken. Peter also attests that this phenomenon is the work of the Holy Spirit of God.
4. Peter begins his first public preaching. He assures the crowd that the Christians are not drunk (to reinforce the idea that many did not understand the languages), but mainly he attests that this strange phenomenon is the work of the Holy Spirit of God (quoting Joel 2:28-32).
5. The 3000 who are led to repent and be baptized as a result of Peter's sermon again demonstrate the power of the Holy Spirit.
6. The power continues as we are told that through the ministry of this Spirit-filled Church, the Lord added to their number

day by day those who were being saved.

What should we conclude from these points? The infilling with the Holy Spirit is not a one-day experience but a continuing reality (Ranaghan, 79-80).

The Holy Spirit is clearly the soul of the New Testament Church. Only because of the Holy Spirit operating in the Church can any person become a part of Jesus Christ, share in His sonship, becoming an heir to the Father. Also, only in the power of the Holy Spirit can any Christian show the love of Christ to others. Without the Day of Pentecost there would be no Church (Ranaghan, 80).

John F. Walvoord declares that on the Day of Pentecost a number of ministries of the Holy Spirit began simultaneously. The new converts in the house of Cornelius were regenerated, indwelt, sealed, and filled with the Spirit at the same moment they were baptized with the Spirit. All of this happened just as it had happened on the Day of Pentecost. Only Christians spoke in tongues, and this phenomenon was enough to justify Peter in concluding that the house of Cornelius was saved (144-145). All those in the house of Cornelius and all those on the Day of Pentecost were prepared to testify of and serve God and His Son Jesus Christ.

Acts chapter 10 gives the direct impression that the Holy Spirit has taken the initiative. There are clear indications that the Spirit of God is at work and Peter knew this when he said, "Who was I that I should withstand God?" (Acts 11:17). Peter was the instrument the Holy Spirit decided to use. It was the Holy Spirit's strategy that selected these men in these places at this particular time to fulfill a specific role in the expansion of the Church. The initiative belonged to the Holy Spirit (Lancaster, "But the Holy Ghost said," 22). Through the book of Acts the same principle is at work: for example, the Holy Spirit directed Philip to leave his work in Samaria and travel to the desert of Gaza; the Holy Spirit instructed him to approach the chariot of the Ethiopian; the Holy Spirit removed Philip after his work was complete (Acts 8:26-39). In the same way, the Holy Spirit called the church at Antioch to set apart Barnabas and Saul "for the work to which I have called them" (Acts 13:2). And then, "being sent out by the Holy Spirit" (v. 4) Barnabas and

Saul follow His directions. When they return to the church at Antioch, they do not report on their work for God, but on "all that God had done with them" (Acts 14:27).

The whole drama of the book of Acts is a reflex of the activity of the Holy Spirit in the lives of yielded disciples and apostles—people who were willing to listen and follow without question the leading of the Holy Spirit in their lives. The Holy Spirit was in charge of things, not simply as a behind-the-scenes observer, but, as Lancaster says, "as the living Representative of Christ who is teaching and inspiring and enabling His followers to fulfill His mission" ("But the . . .," 23). This is exactly what Peter meant when he said, "The Spirit told me to go" (Acts 11:12). Thus the Holy Spirit again sets for the Church of today a precedent—He wants believers to have a sensitivity to the leading of the Holy Spirit so that we will recognize His leading and have the courage to follow Him, even when He cuts across preconceived ideas and does a new thing (Lancaster, 24).

When we read Acts 1:8, "you will receive power . . . you will be my witnesses" we realize the entire program stated in the book of Acts. The business of the people of God in this world is to bear witness to Him. That is the center of Pentecost (Conner, 55). The field of operation is marked out for the disciples. They are to begin where they are, at Jerusalem. Then they are to reach out to places near by, such as Samaria and Judea. Then they will reach out even farther, until finally they get to the ends of the earth—no one is to be left out. Everyone must hear this gospel. The disciples are also told what their equipment is to be: they will receive the power from the Holy Spirit. In fact, He is to be their power (Conner, 56). This was power given by God. The power, in fact, would be God Himself with, upon, and in them. These were unqualified people being sent on a nearly impossible task. But the Spirit would qualify them with all the power necessary to do the task. Pentecost, states Conner, "was the releasing of the redemptive power of Christ among men. Pentecost was the making of the redemptive power of Christ available for men" (61).

What we have, then, in the book of Acts is the power of Christ Himself continuing to work in the lives of men. Peter, in his sermon on the Day of Pentecost, attributes the coming of the Holy Spirit to Christ. The Living Christ was doing this work among them. He had not gone away from them but was still with them working in a new way for the coming of His own Kingdom.

All Christians have the Holy Spirit residing within them as the above scripture clearly points out. Paul says in Romans 8:9 and 11, "You, however, are controlled not by the sinful nature but by the Spirit, if the Spirit of God lives in you. And if anyone does not have the Spirit of Christ, he does not belong to Christ." And he adds in 8:11, "And if the Spirit of him who raised Jesus from the dead is living in you, he who raised Christ from the dead will also give life to your mortal bodies through his Spirit, who lives in you." In other words, if you are saved, then you have the Holy Spirit living in you. If the Spirit is not living in you, then you will not be raised to eternal life. Paul says in I Corinthians 6:19, "Do you not know that your body is a temple of the Holy Spirit, who is in you, whom you have received from God? You are not your own; you were bought with a price." Lampe agrees that, "All Christians are thus partakers of the Spirit, who should 'be filled with the Spirit' (Eph. 5:18) and 'aglow with the Spirit' (Rom. 12:11)" (Lampe, 638). The reason Christians are partakers of the Holy Spirit is that they have received the Holy Spirit when they were saved. They know that Christ lives in them because Christ gave them the Holy Spirit according to 1 John 3:24—"Those who obey his commands live in him, and he in them. And this is how we know that he lives in us: We know it by the Spirit he gave us."

TONGUES IN SAMARIA

Acts 8:4 tells us that Philip the evangelist was led by God to preach salvation to the Samaritans and perform miraculous signs. God delivered these Samaritans of evil spirits and healed numerous paralytics and crippled individuals. Consequently, many Samaritans were saved and baptized in water. We know that the Samaritans technically received the Holy Spirit simply because they were saved. Romans 8:9 says that if people belong to Christ then they have the Holy Spirit. Luke challenges us with his terminology, however, when he says that the Holy Spirit had not come upon them. The problem is that the Samaritans did not manifest the baptism with the Holy Spirit through speaking in tongues at that moment.

That the baptism by the Spirit calls for baptism with the Spirit, John A. Schep explains, is also evidenced by the conversion of the Samaritans (Acts 8:4ff). After Philip preached, many had been converted and baptized. Mighty signs had accompanied the event (38). In Acts 8:14-20, Luke tells us

> When the apostles in Jerusalem heard that Samaria had accepted the word of God, they sent Peter and John to them. When they arrived, they prayed for them that they might receive the Holy Spirit, because the Holy Spirit had not yet come upon any of them; they had simply been baptized into the name of the Lord Jesus. Then Peter and John placed their hands on them, and they received the Holy Spirit. When Simon [the sorcerer] saw that the Spirit was given at the laying on of the apostles' hands, he offered them money and said, 'Give me also this ability so that everyone on whom I lay my hands may receive the Holy Spirit.' Peter answered: 'May your money perish with you, because you thought you could buy the gift of God with money!'

The apostles in Jerusalem, when they learned about the conversions and water baptisms in Samaria, did not consider the experience sufficient. In Acts 8:16 we read that the Samaritans had been baptized in the name of Jesus only. This kind of statement is a clear indication that, according to the apostles, something was lacking. What was lacking became clear when Peter and John went to Samaria.

The problem was resolved when Peter and John laid hands on the Samaritans to manifest the Holy Spirit. Peter and John left, satisfied, because manifestations occurred. Most assuredly, these manifestations included speaking in tongues. Through the laying on of hands, the Samaritans confirmed the baptism with the Holy Spirit by speaking in tongues. Speaking in tongues activates spiritual power and gifts of the Spirit, including the miraculous. This spiritual power, as evident in signs and wonders, occurred in

Samaria; the Samaritans received the baptism with the Holy Spirit through the laying on of hands in approximately AD 39.

Simon the Sorcerer wanted to purchase this power. Simon the Sorcerer must have seen—clearly and obviously—something spectacular. Otherwise he would never have offered money for the power to bring about the same phenomena (Schep, 39). There must have been some sort of miraculous transformation such as happened to the 120 at Pentecost, including speaking in tongues. Peter rebuked Simon the Sorcerer for attempting to purchase the power of God with money. Simon the Sorcerer wanted to market God's power so he could, in turn, make a profit.

How do we know that the people in Samaria spoke with tongues? Acts 8:16 reads that the Samaritans had been baptized in the name of Jesus. Schep points out that some commentators say the Samaritans needed the baptism with the Spirit to assure them, since they had always been outcasts, that they also belonged to the Body of Christ (39). However, there is no scripture to support this theory. Also, to make the Samaritans believe that they belonged to the Church of Christ, a Pentecostal baptism with the Holy Spirit was not at all necessary. They believed in Christ and had been incorporated into Christ's Body by water baptism (I Cor. 12:13). Philip had preached the Messiah of the Jews to them. That was enough evidence to convince them that they were spiritually one in faith with Israel's Messiah. Why did the Samaritans need something over and above faith and regeneration? For the 3,000 on the Day of Pentecost, the Spirit's work in faith and regeneration was not sufficient either. Nor was their being baptized into the body of Christ sufficient. The 3,000 were promised a specific baptism with the Holy Spirit. In Acts chapter 2, "receiving the gift of the Spirit" meant the same as being baptized, or being filled, with the Spirit as the 120 had experienced (Schep, 38).

The apostles realized that these believers in Samaria, as believers elsewhere, needed to be baptized with the Spirit and thereby equipped for powerful service to their Savior and the Church. All Christians must experience the fullness of Pentecost, the baptism with the Holy Spirit with the evidence of speaking in tongues.

P. C. Nelson, in his book *The Baptism in the Spirit*, points out that great numbers—some say 500 million—have received the baptism in the Holy Spirit with the speaking in tongues as evidence. Consequently, people have become interested in studying the Scriptures to see just what this experience is. He adds that some believers point out texts where the speaking in tongues is a definite accompaniment of baptism (e.g., Acts 8:17) while others note that believers did not always speak with tongues upon receiving the Holy Spirit baptism (7).

What have various commentators said about this difference of opinion? We are indebted to P. C. Nelson (5-15) for the following list of comments and interpretations which relate most specifically to the Samaritan's experience of speaking in tongues (the bold is copied from Nelson's list).

1. Matthew Henry (1662-1714)—"they advanced and improved those of them that were sincere. It is said (v. 16) that the Holy Spirit was as yet fallen upon none of them, in those **extraordinary powers** which were conveyed **by the descent** upon the day of Pentecost. . . . none of them were endued with the **gift of tongues, which seems then to have been the most usual, immediate effect of the pouring out of the Spirit.** This was both an eminent sign to them that believe not, and of excellent service to them that did."
2. Adam Clarke (1762-1832)—"they prayed and laid their hands on the disciples and God sent down the gift; so, the blessing **came from God by** the apostles, and **not from the apostles** to the people. But for what purpose was the Holy Spirit given? Certainly not for the sanctification of the souls of the people; this they had upon believing in Christ Jesus. It was the **miraculous gifts** of the Spirit which were given: **the speaking with different tongues** and these **extraordinary qualifications** which were necessary for the successful preaching of the gospel."
3. Joseph Benson (1742-1821)—"Then **laid they their hands on them** . . . Namely after they had prayed for them; and **they received the Holy Ghost**—in answer to the prayers of these apostles; that is, these new converts **spake with**

tongues and performed other extraordinary works."

4. William Burkitt (1650-1703), *Expository Notes on the New Testament*—"they prayed and laid their hands on them and they received the Holy Ghost. Whereby the Holy Ghost is not to be understood the sanctifying graces of the Holy Ghost, which the apostles never did nor could dispense, but the **extraordinary gifts of the Holy Ghost**, the **gift of tongues** and prophecy, and the **power to work miracles**."
5. Charles John Ellicott, *The New Testament Commentary for English Readers* (London, 3rd ed.)—"When Simon saw that through laying on of the apostles' hands . . . . The words imply that the **result was something visible** and **conspicuous**. A change was wrought; and **men spoke with tongues** and prophesied."
6. Hermann Olshausen (1796-1858), *Commentary on the New Testament*—"When Simon perceived the extraordinary effects of the laying on of the apostles' hands, in the gifts which were exhibited, particularly **the speaking in tongues**, he attempted to procure for himself with money the power of communicating the Spirit."
7. Philip Schaff (1819-1893), *International Illustrated Commentary on the New Testament* (New York, 1888)—"the gifts of the Holy Ghost were **plainly visible**. The laying on of the apostles' hands conferred something more than the inward spiritual grace; **outward miraculous gifts of some kind or other were plainly bestowed."**
8. Lutheran Commentary (New York, 1906)—" 'when Simon saw.' Lit., when Simon had seen the effects of the communication of the Holy Ghost, **speaking with tongues**, and the like" (comp.2:4; 10:46sqq.).
9. Albert Barnes (1798-1870), *Notes on the New Testament*—"The phrase, 'the gift of the Holy Ghost' and the 'descent of the Holy Ghost' signified not merely his ordinary influence in converting sinners, but those **extraordinary influences** that attended the first preaching of the gospel—the power of **speaking with new tongues**, the power of working miracles, etc. Acts 19:6."

10. D. D. Whedon (1808-1888), *Commentary on the New Testament* (1890)—"We have here, as at Caesarea and at Ephesus, a **miniature Pentecost**, in which a new inauguration seems to take place by the repetition of the same **charismatic effusions**."
11. Alexander Maclaren (1826-1910), *The Acts in Bible-Class Exposition* (London, 1894)—"The Samaritans had been baptized, but still they lacked the gift of the Spirit. Now the context shows that the gift was **attended with outward effects** which Simon saw, and wished to be able to impart. This fact . . . seems to point to **miraculous gifts** as being principally, if not solely, meant. . . . The visible effects in **miraculous manifestations** is at least probable."
12. H. B. Hacket (1808-1875), *Commentary on the Original Text of the Acts of the Apostles* (1858)—"They **received the Holy Spirit** as the author of the endowments conferred on them. Among these may have been the **gift of tongues** (see 2:4, 10:46) and **also that of prophecy**, as well as the power of working miracles."
13. J. S. Excell, Editor, *The Preacher's Homilitical Commentary*—This shows that the recipients of the Holy Ghost must in some external fashion—probably through **speaking with tongues** or **working miracles**—have indicated their possession of the heavenly gift."
14. M. F. Sadler, *Commentary on the New Testament* (12 vols)—"It is clear that the manifestations of the presence of the Spirit were in outward gifts, such as healing, or **speaking with tongues**. If they had only been gifts of spiritual grace and holiness, Simon would not have discerned them, or would have held them in no account."
15. Henry Alford, *Greek Testament with English Notes*—"'Idon (seeing).' Its effects were therefore visible, and consequently the effect of the laying on of the Apostles' hands was **not the inward, but the outward miraculous gifts** of the Spirit."
16. W. R. Nicoll, *The Expositor's Greek Testament* (with English notes)—"Dr. Hort, who holds that the reception of

the Holy Spirit is here explained as in x. 44 by reference to **the manifestation of the gift of tongues**, points out that the verb is not 'elabon' (the aorist), but 'elambanon," and he therefore renders it, 'showed a succession of signs of the Spirit.'"

17. John Wesley, *Explanatory Notes upon the New Testament* (1752)—"The Holy Ghost—in his **miraculous gifts**? Or his sanctifying graces? Probably both."
18. J. R. Dummelow, *A Commentary on the Holy Bible by Various Writers* (1922) —"'Saw.' It was probable that many upon whom the apostles laid hands received **miraculous gifts**, that Simon, who made his living by working lying wonders, should have desired the power of working genuine ones, is natural enough."
19. Arthur S. Peake, Editor, *Commentary on the Bible* (the commentary on Acts was written by Prof. Allen Menzies of Scotland)—"Simon sees that the Holy Spirit is given through the imposition of the apostles' hands. How does he see it? 10:46 explains, also 19:5; **speaking with tongues seems to have been a normal incident of baptism."**
20. Ernest W. Burch, Notes on the Acts in *The Abingdon Bible Commentary*—"The presence of the Holy Spirit in the community was **evidenced in some very conspicuous way**, for Simon was willing to invest in a power so evident to the beholder."
21. E. J. Bicknell, Notes on Acts, in *A New Commentary on the Holy Scriptures including the Apocrypha* (1928)—"He (Philip) had apparently not attempted to lay hands on them (the new converts in Samaria). Nor had they **displayed the visible signs** of the receiving the Spirit, such as **speaking with tongues**, which was **still expected to mark His coming**. The converts were in the position which the disciples had been in before Pentecost. This was remedied by the laying on of hands, following by some **external sign** of the outpouring of the Spirit."
22. John Albert Bengel (1687-1752), *Gnomon Novi Testamenti* (*Latin Commentary)* (1742)—"It was therefore an apostolic

gift. Philip the evangelist did not have it. Yet Ananias had it in the case of Paul (9:17)."

23. Jamieson, Faussett and Brown, *Critical and Explanatory Commentary*—"As the baptism of adults presupposed 'the renewing of the Holy Ghost' (Titus 3:5-7, I Cor. 12:13), of which the profession of faith had to be taken for evidence, this communication of the Holy Ghost by the laying on of hands was clearly a **superadded** thing; and as it was only occasional, so it was **invariably attended with miraculous manifestations** (see chap 10:44 where it followed Peter's preaching; chap 19:1-7 where it followed the laying on of hands)."
24. Conybeare and Howson, *Life and Epistles of St. Paul*—"The baptized converts, when the apostles laid their hands on them, received **some spiritual gift**, either the power of **working miracles** or of **speaking in tongues**, bestowed upon each of them by Him who 'divideth to every man severally as He will.'"
25. Arthur Cushman McGiffert, *History of Christianity in the Apostolic Age* (1890)—"It is clear . . . that the descent of the Holy Spirit upon the Samaritan disciples was attended with certain **visible and audible phenomena**, as was common in the apostolic age. . . . The gift of the Spirit meant to the early Christians in general not the inspiring and controlling power of the entire Christian life, as it did to Paul, but the **ability to speak with tongues, or to prophesy or to do some other startling, uncommon and miraculous thing**. And so the evidence of the Spirit's presence was commonly found in these early days in such marvelous manifestations, which seem to have been very frequently witnessed." In a footnote he adds, "the disciples who received the Spirit made the impression even upon unbelievers of being in possession of a power outside and above themselves. Simon would never have offered money for a power that produced effects which might as easily be produced in other ways and which gave no clear indication of supernatural influence" (2nd ed., pp. 98, 99).

26. The Modernist Shailer Matthews and his Associate Professor George Holley Gilbert, who wrote the "Interpretive Comments in Acts" in the series in Matthews' *Bible for Home and School*, agree with the commentators cited. Dr. Gilbert wrote that the "baptism in the name of Jesus was **not considered a complete equipment** for the Christian life. It marked the **first stage**." The verses in Acts 8 suggest that "there was some visible manifestation on the part of those on whom the hands of the apostles had been laid. We may think of ecstatic speech or of some sign done by those who had received the gift of the Spirit" (see 6:5, 8; 8:6). He adds that "Unless the gift of the Spirit had been accompanied with some extraordinary manifestation, something that could be seen, Simon would have had no grounds for making the offer of money."

We have quoted at some length from these various commentators to indicate that there is clear evidence as to the experience in Samaria. The following conclusions should especially be observed from the preceding opinions and commentaries (from P. C. Nelson, 17-18):

1. All the commentators quoted agree that there was some visible, outward, miraculous manifestation or evidence of the presence of the Spirit.
2. Nearly all of them mention the speaking with tongues as almost certainly the manifestation, or one of the manifestations.
3. All agree that this experience was something in addition to, and subsequent to, the regeneration of these Samaritans.
4. None of them assert that this can in any way be interpreted as sanctification, and some of them specifically declare that such an interpretation is untenable.
5. Most of them agree that the gift here mentioned was not for a select few but for all the true believers.

Several great expositors of the Book of Acts mention the working of miracles of some kind, or the manifestation of one of the spiritual gifts. Then why insist on tongues as the outward evidence at Samaria and also in our time? Why not the gift of wisdom, of knowledge, of faith, of discernment or interpretation? Note the following points.

1. In each case where a manifestation is named in connection with the Baptism with the Holy Spirit, tongues are named—at Pentecost, at Caesarea, at Ephesus.
2. Any outward sign or evidence of the infilling with the Holy Spirit should be easily recognized by the person himself and by those present. It should be evident any time and always—to conform to the Bible pattern.
3. The other gifts of the Spirit (mentioned above before #1) would not be discernable to the audience nor to the person who had received the Baptism with the Holy Spirit—they all require special circumstances to be evident. The manifestation of tongues is possible anytime, anywhere, and whether any one is present or a thousand are present. P. C. Nelson states, "There is a divine wisdom in selecting this manifestation as the sign of the incoming of the Holy Spirit. And what could be more appropriate or thrilling? 'Tongues are for a sign'" (27).

TONGUES IN CAESAREA

Cornelius, a Roman centurion, was a God-fearing Gentile who lived in Caesarea. According to Acts 10, he was not saved. At this time, Peter was in Joppa. At 3:00 p.m., Cornelius had a vision in which an angel of God told him to send men to Joppa to bring Peter back to his house in Caesarea. The very next day, Cornelius' servants approached the house in Joppa where Peter was staying.

As Cornelius' servants approached the house, Peter was waiting for lunch to be prepared. Suddenly, Peter had a vision to prepare him to receive the Gentiles. In his vision, Peter saw a sheet coming down from above being held by the four corners. In this sheet was every kind of unclean animal, none of which would have been acceptable for Jews to eat (unkosher). As the vision continued, Peter heard the voice of God saying to kill and eat these animals. Peter was an orthodox Jew and refused to disobey the Law of Moses. Peter heard this command three times in his vision.

But since the Law said that the Messiah may perform a midrash (that is to change laws and customs), and since Peter knew Jesus was the Messiah, he finally realized that this vision was really of God and that it was in obedience to God that he could accept Gentiles and associate with them. Immediately when the vision was over, the Gentile men arrived and Peter went with them. Peter took with him fellow believing Jews as witnesses and character references since other Jews would not otherwise know why Peter broke the Mosaic Law.

Peter went into Cornelius' house, which was filled with Gentiles, and began preaching the gospel. He preached how Jesus, the Jewish Messiah, died for their sins, but was resurrected from the dead and ascended into heaven. Acts 10:44-47 says, "While Peter was still speaking these words, the Holy Spirit came on all who heard the message. The circumcised believers who had come with Peter were astonished that the gift of the Holy Spirit had been poured out even on the Gentiles. For the believers heard them speaking in tongues and praising God. Then Peter said, 'Can anyone keep these people from being baptized with water?'" This method of receiving the baptism with the Holy Spirit was through the sovereign will of God and occurred in AD 41.

Never before had Gentiles received the Holy Spirit. This event became known as the Gentile Pentecost. Rumors of this event spread to the church in Jerusalem. Jewish believers and elders were concerned about Peter's reputation since he broke the Law of Moses. But Peter took his witnesses with him to Jerusalem to explain to the Jewish elders that God gave him a vision in which he was told that he must accept the Gentiles. He said in Acts 11:15-18, "As I began to speak, the Holy Spirit came on them as he had come on us at the beginning. Then I remembered what the Lord had said, 'John baptized with water, but you will be baptized with the Holy Spirit.' So if God gave them the same gift as he gave us who believed in the Lord Jesus Christ, who was I to think that I could oppose God! When they heard this, they had no further objections and praised God, saying, 'So then, God has even granted the Gentiles repentance unto life.'"

TONGUES IN EPHESUS

Acts 19:1-7 provides the last text on the method in which believers in the New Testament received the baptism with the Holy Spirit. The passage reads thus:

> While Apollos was at Corinth, Paul took the road through the interior and arrived at Ephesus. There he found some disciples and asked them, 'Did you receive the Holy Spirit when you believed?' They answered, 'No, we have not even heard that there is a Holy Spirit.' So Paul asked, 'Then what baptism did you receive?' 'John's baptism,' they replied. Paul said, 'John's baptism was a baptism of repentance. He told the people to believe in the one coming after him, that is, in Jesus.' On hearing this, they were baptized into the name of the Lord Jesus. When Paul placed his hands on them, the Holy Spirit came on them, and they spoke in tongues and prophesied. There were about twelve men in all.

This case study most closely resembles that of the Samaritans in Acts 8, at least in the methodology in which believers received the baptism with the Holy Spirit. The method in common is the laying on of hands. The disposition of these Jewish men was that they knew very little about Jesus. They were disciples of John the Baptist as were many Jews around the Roman Empire. Their spiritual experience was that they were penitent men as illustrated by receiving the ritual Jewish baptism, as administered by John the Baptist. Jewish baptism symbolized repentance from sin. Followers of Jesus Christ were to receive Jewish baptism, but in the name of the Father, Son, and Holy Spirit, demonstrating their salvation experience. They did not know about the Holy Spirit. So Paul taught them what Jesus Christ did for them through his life, crucifixion, resurrection, and the giving of the Holy Spirit. Consequently, these Ephesians were saved, received the Holy Spirit, spoke in tongues, and prophesied. They received the baptism with the Holy Spirit through the laying on of hands in AD 54.

It is interesting to observe that in Acts 2, the believers simultaneously received the Holy Spirit and spoke in tongues. In Acts 8, the Samaritans 1) were saved, 2) were baptized in water, and then 3) spoke in tongues. In Acts 10, the household of Cornelius 1) simultaneously was saved and spoke in tongues, and then 2) were baptized in water. In Acts 19, the Ephesian men 1) were saved, 2) received Christian water baptism, and then 3) spoke in tongues, like the Samaritans. We can learn from these examples that God cannot be limited by man in His operations through His Spirit. It is not our place to tell God how He must work. Our duty is to pray with believers to receive the baptism with the Holy Spirit, and commit the results into God's hands.

It was absolutely essential—primarily because of the intense mission it had to accomplish—that the early Church be a Church of Spirit-filled believers. Schep points out that repeatedly in the book of Acts we see the importance of this Spirit infilling or power-giving baptism (40-41). Cornelius and his friends had been baptized with the Holy Spirit even before they received water baptism. Peter accepted this Holy Spirit baptism as evidence that he was working with true believers even though they had been pagans. Peter accepted the fact that baptism with the Spirit was the privilege of true believers only, no one else. Paul's conversion was significant too. Paul certainly received the gift of tongues. He recorded in I Corinthians 14:18 what an important place tongues occupied in his own life. That Paul was specially baptized with the Holy Spirit proves that this baptism is intended for all believers. Paul was a Jew. But Paul was not among the 120 on the Day of Pentecost. If such Holy Spirit baptism had been only for the Day of Pentecost, Paul could not have received it. Yet we know he did receive it.

Additionally, the disciples that Paul found at Ephesus on his third missionary journey (Acts 19:1-7) had not received, nor even heard of, the Pentecostal outpouring of the Holy Spirit. Paul gave them instruction in the work of Pentecost, and when they believed, they were baptized and incorporated into the Church of Christ (Schep, 41). If it is true that a Christian needs the Holy Spirit only as the One who brings works of faith and regeneration, then Paul should have been content. Especially since this took place 20 years after Pentecost, he should have been content with the people's progress. Yet Paul was not satisfied until these men had received the Pentecostal baptism with the Holy Spirit. Obviously, then, Paul considered such a Spirit baptism as a separate work from redemption but an essential work of empowerment for all Christians.

When Paul asked the question, "Did you receive the Holy Spirit when you believed?" he indicated his own belief that the baptism with the Holy Spirit was a normal post-conversion experience for all believers. Paul considered it a definite experience that one could identify and could know whether or not one had received it (Schep, 41).

Luke, then, throughout Acts, teaches a post-conversion Spirit baptism, granted first to the 120 and subsequently to many others at various times. The subsequent baptisms indicate that the experience was for all believers. Some deny that the baptism is meant for all believers because Luke does not record such a Spirit baptism for all conversions. For example, no mention is made of a Spirit baptism for the Ethiopian eunuch (Acts 8:26ff). Nor was a baptism mentioned in the reports of conversions during Paul's missionary journeys, except for the twelve men at Ephesus.

But such an argument is based on what is not stated rather than on what is stated (Schep, 42). Therefore, it could not possibly invalidate conclusions from what is clearly stated. In other places in his writings, Luke omits things that had undoubtedly taken place, simply because they were self-evident events or facts. If Luke considered Spirit baptisms a matter of course for those converted during Paul's missionary journeys, there would be no need to describe such baptisms. In fact, Schep points out that in most of these conversions from Paul's missionary journeys, Luke does not even report that the converts were baptized with water (43).

According to John R. W. Stott, Acts 8 and Acts 19 show something unusual. The twelve men in chapter 19, Stott says, do not appear to have been Christians at all. They are called "disciples," but they were really disciples of John the Baptist. True, Paul did ask them if they had received the Holy Spirit when they believed (v. 2), showing that Paul thought they were Christians. But their reply to him indicates that he was probably mistaken. Note these points:

they had never heard of the Holy Spirit (v. 2); they had to be told that "the one who was to come," was in fact Jesus (v. 4); Paul not only laid hands on them but had to first baptize them into "the name of Jesus" (v. 5) (19). Stott asks, "Can those who have never heard of the Holy Spirit nor been baptized into Christ, nor even apparently believed in him, be called Christians? I think not" (19). These disciples, then, are not typical of the average Christian believer today.

Philip, in Acts 8:5-17, continues Stott, preached the gospel in Samaria where many had believed and been baptized. No question but that these were Christian believers. So why did the apostles at Jerusalem decide to send Peter and John? There is no other occasion where evangelistic work had to be inspected by two apostles. For example, no apostle was sent to check out the salvation and baptism of the Ethiopian eunuch at the end of the same chapter (vv. 26-40). Stott believes that since this was the first time the gospel had been preached outside Jerusalem, God withheld the baptism of the Samaritan believers until two of the leading apostles came down to confirm and acknowledge the genuineness of the Samaritans' conversion (20).

The special manifestations of the Holy Spirit in Acts, then, are these: speaking in tongues (2:4, 10:46, 19:6), praising God (10:46), bold proclamation (2:11, 4:8, 4:31), power in confrontation (6:10, 13:9), new Christian prophecy (2:17-18, 11:28, 20:23, 21:4, 21:11), vision (7:55), and guidance for the church or for individuals (8:29, 10:19, 11:12, 13:2). Also, at times, the Spirit sent (13:4), forbade (16:6-7), or bound (20:22) people on certain occasions, and also placed people as overseers of the believers (20:28). Particularly noticeable is the emphasis on the ideas of communication, proclamation, and guidance (Heron, 43-44).

CHAPTER VII

TONGUES IN THE EPISTLES

"In St. Paul's Epistles the Holy Spirit is mentioned nearly 120 times," states Denney in his article "Holy Spirit," in *Dictionary of Christ and the Gospels.* Additionally, he adds that the Holy Spirit "may be said to have a prominence and importance which it has nowhere else in the New Testament" (p. 738 cited in Thomas, 24). The work of the Holy Spirit held so large a place in the early church that no Apostolic letter to the churches could ignore the Holy Spirit altogether (Swete, *Holy Spirit*, 226).

Paul teaches about the relation of the Holy Spirit to individuals as well as the relation of the Holy Spirit to the universal Church (Swete, Article "Holy Spirit," 410). For the Holy Spirit's work in individuals, note that the Apostle Paul repeatedly speaks of the personal pronoun both in the first and second persons (me/mine and you/your) when he refers to the work of the Holy Spirit in those he writes to. For example, he tells Timothy "Guard the good deposit that was entrusted to you—guard it with the help of the Holy Spirit who lives in us" (2 Tim. 1:14). The doctrine of the Holy Spirit in the Church is based on the fact that the Holy Spirit is in individuals. Because He lives in individuals, He is also in the community (Thomas, 32). The Church has the Holy Spirit only because individuals who comprise the Church have Him indwelling them first.

It is through the Epistles of Paul that we derive so many functional designations of names or titles for the Holy Spirit. The Holy Spirit is called the Spirit that dwells in us (Rom. 8:11), the Spirit of grace (Heb. 10:29), the Spirit of wisdom and revelation in the knowledge of the Lord Jesus Christ (Eph. 1:17), the Spirit of adoption (Rom. 8:15), the Spirit of life (Rom. 8:2), the Spirit of meekness (Gal. 6:1), the Spirit of power, and of love, and of a sound mind (2 Tim. 1:7) (Smeaton, *The Doctrine of the Holy Spirit*, p. 58, qtd. Thomas, 28). The Holy Spirit is the source, principle, and support of the spiritual life. Paul's Epistles also refer to the Holy Spirit as the Spirit of sonship (Rom. 8:15), and liberty (2 Cor. 3:17), the Spirit of holiness (Gal. 5:22), the Spirit of heirship (Eph. 1:14), and the guarantee of our resurrection (Rom. 8:11) (Thomas, 29).

In Paul's writings there is a rich conception and deep exploration of the nature of the Spirit, including the activity of the Holy Spirit and His connection with Jesus Christ (Heron, 44). The Holy Spirit is the center of Paul's theology and teachings. Paul speaks of contrasts—of two modes of reality—such as light and darkness, faith and works, life and death, righteousness and sin, divine wisdom and human foolishness. These antitheses all center around Jesus Christ himself (Heron, 45). The apostle Paul presents the Holy Spirit as having activity wide and all-encompassing, from justification to the end times, from faith and prayer to ethical behavior and kinship with God the Father (Heron, 46). The Holy Spirit as the active and transforming presence of God cannot be separated from the crucified and risen Jesus Christ on whom the Holy Spirit rested (47). According to St. Paul, no one comprehends the thoughts of God except the Spirit of God (I Cor. 2:11). And Paul adds, in I Cor. 2:12, "We have received not the spirit of the world but the Spirit who is from God." The Holy Spirit is the "inner dynamic of the life of faith" (Heron, 46).

According to W. T. Davison, *The Indwelling Spirit*, the heart of the Pauline doctrine of the Holy Spirit can be summed up thus: the goal of the Holy Spirit is the possession of the spirits of believers—the purification, control, guidance, assurance, and transformation of those human spirits of believers—by the indwelling Holy Spirit for the glory of Christ. That is His goal and purpose. "We are in the Spirit if He is in us. And without the Spirit of Christ Himself at work within us, we can do nothing" (Davison, 77, qtd. Thomas, 37).

Paul begins his speaking about the Holy Spirit by reminding us that the Holy Spirit is the gift of God. In Ephesians Paul prays that God may give the Spirit to His people (Eph. 1:17). However, Paul also speaks of the Holy Spirit in another way, observes William Barclay—a way not usually used by other writers. In Galatians 3:5 he speaks of God *ministering* His Holy Spirit to us. Also, in Philippians 1:19 Paul speaks of the *supply* of the Spirit of Jesus Christ. Through these words we get the idea that the Holy Spirit is a means of equipping us for the part we will play in furthering God's Kingdom. Through the Holy Spirit God cares for us and provides for us. But also through the Holy Spirit God equips us for the battle against sin and Satan, against the powers of this world and of darkness (*Promise*, 65).

The Apostle Paul distinguishes the Gifts of the Holy Spirit from the gift of the Holy Spirit given to all believers who receive the baptism with the Holy Spirit. Peter told the crowd he was preaching to on the Day of Pentecost that they would receive the gift of the Holy Spirit (Acts 2). He refers specifically to the baptism with the Holy Spirit which the 120 had just received with speaking in tongues as the initial evidence. The gifts of the Spirit, however, are given by the Holy Spirit as a part of His ministry in the Church. Ralph Riggs explains that only after one has received the Baptism with the Holy Spirit does the Holy Spirit begin to function in the believer in His own right as the Holy Spirit of God (118). Gifts then—such as prophecy, wisdom, knowledge, discerning of spirits, faith, miracles, healings, tongues and interpretation of tongues—are manifestations of the Spirit within the believer, a separate function from the infilling of the believer in baptism.

Gifts of the Spirit are given to people so they may grow in the fruit of the Spirit. The fruit of the Spirit is the harvest of God's sowing within a person. "The fruit of the Spirit are the characteristics of Jesus" (Ranaghan, 133). The Baptism with the Holy Spirit results in the Christian being given extra growth in the fruit of the Spirit—"to possess the fruit of the Spirit is to be Christlike" (133). Bill Bright agrees that spiritual gifts can be a vibrant part of our lives, but he warns that we should never place the emphasis on the gifts rather than on the Holy Spirit and Christ Himself. The gifts of the Spirit, Bright states, "are given for glorifying Christ in love, for equipping the saint in love, and for unifying the body of Christ in love" (193).

Though Paul emphasizes the gifts of the Holy Spirit in the lives of individual believers, he also teaches how those gifts should be used. The gifts undoubtedly bring joy and fulfillment to the individual, but Paul stressed their role in "building up and strengthening the church. They are not private gifts in which the Christian may glory" states Wayne Ward, but "rather, they are God's gift to the church, for His glory" (12). If the church could remember that the glory is God's, not man's, there would be more accomplished through them. Also, the gifts are corporate gifts, given for the blessing and edification of the entire church, not for private use only (Ward, 12). The Baptism with the Holy Spirit, on the other hand, though there are some corporate benefits, is primarily for the personal use of the one who has received; the baptism strengthens one's own relationship with the Holy Spirit—the Holy Spirit will work in each person individually and personally.

The Epistles clearly declare that the Holy Spirit is essential to give us power to fight the spiritual warfare we face everyday. All believers need the fullness of the Holy Spirit, the baptism with the Holy Spirit, if we are to complete the task given us. We have been "sent out to accomplish a spiritual task, and this is not possible without spiritual ability" (Duffield, 309). There is no substitute for the power of the Holy Spirit in us.

Paul's letters indicate that the Holy Spirit has a special part to play in man's relationship to God. Through the Holy Spirit, God's love comes to us (Rom. 5:5). Through the Holy Spirit man has access to God (Eph. 2:18). Through the Holy Spirit we are adopted into the family of God (Rom. 8:14-16). The Holy Spirit puts into man's heart the desire to be part of the family of God in the first place. The Holy Spirit assures us of our welcome into that new family. The Holy Spirit brings us out of the physical world of sin and into the spiritual world of God (69-70). Paul presents the Holy Spirit as bringing the greatest gifts of the Christian life. Righteousness comes through the Spirit (Rom. 14:17). We are incapable of righteous living on our own. Only with the daily help of the Holy Spirit can we find victory over sin and self. Only through the Holy Spirit can the fruit of the Spirit grow in us (Thomas, 73).

Though the church already lives in the power of the Holy Spirit, the old carnal nature of man has not yet been destroyed, and we are caught in the tension between the Holy Spirit and the flesh. The Holy Spirit's praying in us is a kindling of a hope for what is not yet—for the completion of God's Kingdom and God's purposes on earth. "The present gift of the Spirit is a 'pledge'. . . a 'first-fruits' or 'down payment' (Rom. 8:23). This hope points beyond the resurrection, . . . when the whole creation 'will be set free from bondage'" (Heron, 50-51). This dynamic is fundamental to the work of the Holy Spirit. The power of God drives towards the end of history and carries us toward the hope we received from the resurrection of Jesus Christ.

The indwelling of the Holy Spirit gives believers this new spiritual life, the mark of a New Testament Christian. "You, however, are controlled not by the sinful nature but by the Spirit, if the Spirit of God lives in you" (Rom. 8:9). Paul's letter to the Romans lets us know that the most comprehensive definition of a Christian is that he is filled with the Holy Spirit. And when we are filled with the Holy Spirit, we are temples in whom the Holy Spirit dwells (I Cor. 6:19) (Duffield, 277).

The Holy Spirit inspires and guides our prayer life. The intercession He leads us in (Rom. 8:26-27), when we don't know how to pray as we ought to, is not intercession far away in some distant heavenly place. His intercession is in our own hearts (Conner, 107). Frank M. Boyd, in *The Spirit Works Today*, explains that Paul gives two main uses of tongues (131): in prayer and in the church. In I Cor. 14:2, 14, 15 the apostle Paul tells us that "he who speaks in a tongue speaks to God." Thus our prayer language, or tongues, is a language for direct communication between the believer and God Himself. Also, in I Cor. 14:22 Paul points out that the Church is edified, built up, by tongues in the church services (especially if there is an interpretation), but also that in the Church tongues are a sign to the unbeliever (132).

Walter Thomas Conner, in *The Work of the Holy Spirit: A Treatment of the Biblical Doctrine of the Divine Spirit,* adds that the indwelling of the Holy Spirit, within the Spirit-filled believer, gives the church the power to survive (132). Paul speaks of the Christians as the temple or sanctuary of God (I Cor. 3:16-17, 6:19-20). Only because the Holy Spirit dwells in Christians is it possible for them to be constituted as a temple of God. In fact, Conner points out that the word used for "sanctuary" in the two passages in I Corinthians is the same term used for the inner sanctuary or the Holy Place where only the priests could enter and the Most Holy Place where only the High Priest could enter (132). Jesus applies this same term to His own body when He says, "Destroy this temple and in three days I will raise it up" (John 2:19).

In the Old Testament, God met his people in the tabernacle and spoke to them there. Paul emphasizes the idea that if the Spirit of God dwells in his people, they are his habitation. The Holy Spirit of God living in God's people makes them God's people, God's habitation (Conner, 133). The Presence of the Holy Spirit in us brings a constant awareness of the presence of God. The Spirit dwells in the Christian (Rom. 8:9, 11; I Cor. 3:16-17). Because the Christian is filled with the Holy Spirit, the Christian is the temple of the Holy Spirit (I Cor. 6:19)—the Christian himself is the Holy of Holies in which the Spirit of God lives (Thomas, 79).

Paul connected the Holy Spirit in believers' lives with ethical conduct. As he taught right conduct, he also emphasized that the Holy Spirit was in us to help us to achieve that kind of conduct. The Holy Spirit, because He is holy, creates an increasing sensitiveness in the Christian's heart toward sin. He gives, also, an increasing maturity of judgment as to what is right and what is wrong (Conner, 111). But Conner gives encouragement by stating that the Holy Spirit also gives the Christian an increasing ability to overcome sin (112).

Guy P. Duffield mentions a significant reason for believing the Holy Spirit no longer lives in those who sin. When Adam lost his spiritual life, through disobedience to God, many believe he lost the indwelling presence of the Holy Spirit (277). God had warned that death would follow disobedience to His Word (Gen. 2:17). As a result of this sin, Adam was in spiritual darkness or living with a lack of the Holy Spirit (277). Myer Pearlman, in his book *Knowing the Doctrines of the Bible*, clarifies the Apostle Paul's teachings as to why such sin would separate a person from the Holy Spirit: "In relation to understanding, the unconverted cannot know the things of the Spirit of God (I Cor. 2:14); in relation to worship, he cannot call Jesus Lord (I Cor. 12:3); as regards practice, he cannot please God (Rom. 8:8); in regard to character, he cannot bear spiritual fruit (John 15:4); in regards to faith, he cannot receive the Spirit of truth (John 14:17)" (306).

Paul also stresses the work of the Holy Spirit in empowering the believer for a life of ministry and service for God's kingdom. Ministry and service are always pictured in the Scriptures as being done through the power of the Holy Spirit (Duffield, 281) rather than through the power of man himself: "Not by might, nor by power, but by my spirit, says the Lord Almighty" (Zech. 4:6). The baptism with the Holy Spirit is given especially so that men would have the spiritual power necessary to carry on the ministry of the Kingdom of God.

Paul also taught that the Holy Spirit gives power for preaching the Word of God. Paul says, "My message and my preaching were not with wise and persuasive words, but with a demonstration of the Spirit's power" (I Cor. 2:4). We saw the same kind of power come to Peter on the Day of Pentecost (Acts 5:32) when he got up to preach to the crowd—the supernatural power to preach that comes with the baptism with the Holy Spirit. Effective preaching of the gospel must be under the anointing of the Holy Spirit (Duffield, 283)—only the Holy Spirit can convict men of sin and make men realize their need for spiritual transformation. Unless the message is given under the power of the Holy Spirit, the preaching is in vain.

In order to bring ourselves under the control of the living person Jesus Christ, we must realize that He is available to transform us only through the immediate power of the Holy Spirit. The Spirit's function is to bring us under the control of Christ Himself (Conner, 104).

CHAPTER VIII

THE MEANING OF TONGUES

Should we insist that all speak with tongues when they are baptized with the Holy Spirit? Most commentators mention some form of miracle or manifestation of one of the other gifts of the Spirit as accompaniment to the infilling with the Holy Spirit. Tongues were the outward evidence at Samaria, but are they necessarily the only clear or universal outward manifestation in our time? Many believe tongues are only one possible manifestation to verify that one has been baptized with the Holy Spirit.

Looking closely, though, we note that in each case where a manifestation is specifically mentioned in connection with the infilling with the Holy Spirit, tongues are named. This is true of Pentecost, Caesarea, and Ephesus. At Pentecost, they "began to speak with tongues as the Spirit gave them utterance" (Acts 2:4); at Caesarea, they spoke with tongues and magnified God (Acts 10:46); at Ephesus they "spoke with tongues and prophesied" (Acts 19:6) (Nelson, 26). Tongues would be a sign easily recognized by the person himself and by the other people present at the time. Other gifts that could possibly accompany the baptism with the Holy Spirit are not easily identified by others or even by the person himself. For example, wisdom can be manifested only when there is a special occasion for it. The same would be true of the gift of knowledge, of faith, of miracles, of discernment, and of the interpretation of tongues. Miracles, too, were given to meet some specific need, not just to show that the believer could work miracles. There could not have been enough specific needs at Pentecost for 120 to perform enough so that all could identify the miracles as evidence of a baptism. The same is true of healing. With tongues, the manifestation of the Spirit is possible anytime, anywhere, and whether any one or a thousand are present (Nelson, 26-27). Tongues, then, are an appropriate sign for the incoming of the Holy Spirit.

The tongues spoken in the New Testament were not always intelligible to those who were present and heard the language. At Pentecost those who spoke with tongues were understood by each other and by those who heard them speak. At Corinth, though, the messages in tongues required interpretation (note especially I Cor. 14:2-9, 13, 18, 19, 27, 28). Conybeare and Howson remark that, "First, it was not a knowledge of foreign languages, as is often supposed; we never read of it being exercised for the conversion of foreign nations nor (except on the day of Pentecost alone) for that of individual foreigners" (chap. XIII, 354, quoted in Nelson, 28).

Are messages in tongues in our times sometimes understood by persons present? Not always, of course, but certainly sometimes. P. C. Nelson cites a specific case that makes the point clearly (28):

> At a reception given by the Dean of Women [Southwestern Bible School, Enid, Oklahoma], after a spiritual program had been rendered, and opportunity was afforded for those who desired to speak out their hearts' gratitude to God for His manifold mercies to do so, some gave messages in tongues and some interpretations. Among them was a student, Miss Helen Armentrout, who was preparing to go as a missionary to India. The message came in power, but only one person present understood it. This was Miss Mollie Baird, a former missionary to India, then home on furlough, and that year teacher of missions in Southwestern. She broke down and wept, saying, 'This message was in Kurdu, one of the languages of northern India, a language which I learned there. I understood it. It was a personal message from the Lord to myself. He commands me to return to India.' This she did and soon both of

them were laboring for Christ in that needy field.

To those who hear the message but do not understand, tongues is a supernatural manifestation, a sign of the presence of God. It frequently strikes listeners with awe. The interpretation of tongues will often bring people to conviction or to repentance. P. C. Nelson gives a specific example showing the power of speaking in tongues:

> At El Dorado, Arkansas, the author [Nelson] was conducting a campaign, and some were being converted daily, but no great number in any one service. One night as he was about to preach, very unexpectedly a young man gave forth a lengthy message in tongues. It came in the power of the Spirit. This was interpreted by a Sister in the chorus. This was followed by another message and interpretation, and in like manner still another message, which was interpreted in the power of the Spirit. In a few words those desiring to seek the face of God for salvation were asked to come to the altar. Immediately about thirty came forward, fell on their knees and began to confess their sins and ask God's pardon. Among those who responded was a young physician, and others who had remained untouched by the preaching of the Word of God. Those who refuse to believe facts like these should take the trouble to investigate before making sweeping denials, lest haply they should be 'found even to fight against God' (Acts 5:39) (Nelson, 29-30).

Since we today are still in the church age, why shouldn't speaking in tongues, therefore, continue at the present time? If it should not continue at the present time, where is the historical line drawn? Where in scripture did the theological change take place? Some people argue that Satan speaks in tongues. The devil does not speak in tongues. If he did and if this were an issue with which we should be concerned, Paul would have addressed this issue in Scripture. But nowhere at any time did Paul address this issue in Scripture.

Therefore, we don't need to be concerned about it. Some people argue that Jesus did not speak in tongues, so we shouldn't either. It may be true that Jesus did not speak in tongues. He didn't need to. He had full communication with the Father and knew how to pray. Also, speaking in tongues is a New Testament Church phenomenon. Jesus' earthly life pre-dated the era of the New Testament early church. Consequently, the fact that He did not speak in tongues cannot be used as an argument against His followers' speaking in tongues during the church age. Also, Jesus is the one who told His disciples that one of the signs following those who believe would be speaking in new tongues.

Tongues are God's idea and operation, states Ralph Riggs (162). Before the Day of Pentecost had come, salvation had been primarily among the one nation of the Jews. The mother tongue, then, was sufficient as a means of presenting the message of regeneration. On the Day of Pentecost, however, salvation would become available to all people and all nations. Therefore, other tongues are chosen by the Holy Spirit as a necessary new vehicle through which to speak (163). Riggs believes that the changing of language through which the Holy Spirit chooses to speak is indicative of the fact that "now He wants His message to go to all nations, to the ends of the earth. Matt. 28:19; Acts 1:8" (163). Since that day, the Holy Spirit dwells in and enlivens the entire community of believers, regardless of nation, tribe, or tongue.

On the Day of Pentecost when the crowd heard the 120 speaking in languages familiar to the listeners if not to the speakers, the crowd admitted that they heard the 120 "speak in our own tongues the wonderful works of God" (Acts 2:5-11). These people had not yet heard Peter's sermon. Later Peter preached to them in the regularly spoken language. But since they had heard the 120 speaking in many languages, all giving praise to God, the tongues were a most convincing sign to unbelievers. The Holy Spirit, then, used the tongues as a sign (Riggs, 164).

Donald Gee, in his well-known defense of speaking with tongues titled *All With One Accord,* states that it was the "linking together of speaking with tongues and the baptism in the Holy Spirit that sparked off the Pentecostal revival" (30). Out of that experience emerged the belief that speaking with tongues is the "initial evidence" of the baptism with the Holy Spirit. Gee, in defense of tongues as the initial evidence, says "It has made seeking and then receiving the baptism in the Spirit a definite experience that can be marked off as to place and time of reception" (30).

Donald Gee boldly states, "Audacious though it may sound to affirm it, I believe that an unanswerable case can be made out, if we stand on the Scriptures alone, for the doctrine that there is a manifest initial evidence Divinely ordained for the Baptism in the Holy Spirit, . . . that evidence being speaking with tongues" (*Pentecost*, 17). Had the sign of tongues appeared only at Pentecost, there could have been considerable doubt that tongues were intended for a perpetual sign, explains Frederick Bruner (81). But when the Gentiles experienced the same sign, and when a group of Ephesians experienced the same sign a few years later, and when many Pentecostals have experienced it during many centuries later, then there seems little doubt that a pattern is established for all Christians (Bruner, 82).

That the Holy Spirit chose the tongue to evidence His coming seems especially reasonable. Brandt points out that since the tongue is the most unruly member (according to James 3:8), therefore to indicate complete surrender by man and complete control by the Holy Spirit, the tongue is the most logical member to use (4) as a sign of that surrender.

Other reasons for speaking in tongues as an initial evidence for receiving the baptism with the Holy Spirit include the following. First, tongues speaking gives the believer an unshakeable assurance that the Spirit is truly in his life. John Sherrill asked Pentecostals what tongues did for them, and the main answer he received was "assure me that I have been baptized in the Holy Ghost" (79). Second, tongues speaking gives the baptism with the Holy Spirit a tangibility, even a physicality that balances the spiritual experience; for example, Bruner explains that "Tongues speaking, by being at the same time a highly spiritual and a highly physical experience, transforms the coming of the Holy Spirit into a knowable, clear, and datable experience, manifest in time and space" (84). Donald Gee adds that tongues "made the Baptism in the Holy Spirit a definite experience. Nothing was left to a vague 'taking by faith' with a hoped for change in character and power" (Conference speech, 10). And third, the speaking in tongues assures the observing church that the experience is authentic. There needed to be some sign to preserve the church from deception. The scriptural sign is tongues (Bruner, 85).

CHAPTER IX

NECESSITY OF RECEIVING THE BAPTISM WITH THE HOLY SPIRIT

P. C. Nelson points out that many believers, experiencing the joy of receiving the baptism in the Spirit, decide that this baptism is a luxury, an added benefit, rather than a necessity (41). The Word of God, however, emphasizes the necessity of this experience of baptism with the Holy Spirit. Jesus commanded His disciples to tarry until they were endued with power from on high (Luke 24:49): "I am going to send you what my Father has promised; but stay in the city until you have been clothed with power from on high." Later, Jesus commanded them, Do not leave Jerusalem, but wait for the gift my Father promised, ... in a few days you will be baptized with the Holy Spirit" (Acts 1:4, 5). Such commands show that the Baptism with the Holy Spirit was not a luxury but a necessity.

Jesus began His ministry and His miracles after the Holy Spirit came upon Him at His baptism by John the Baptist. Peter was transformed on the Day of Pentecost. The gifts of God now rested on him; tongues, prophecy, healing, faith, miracles, boldness and wisdom to preach God's word were his daily equipment from then on. Just as weapons and various implements of warfare are powerful in the hands of trained soldiers and will help the military win a battle, so God has all this equipment in the Holy Spirit for His warriors of the Cross (Riggs, 82).

Scripture gives several reasons that believers should be or must be filled with the baptism with the Holy Spirit. The importance of believers being filled can be seen from the following points with supporting scriptural references (taken from Nelson, 41-48).

1. **Jesus Himself was anointed with the Spirit before He began His public ministry**. "As soon as Jesus was baptized, he went up out of the water. At that moment heaven was opened, and he saw the Spirit of God descending like a dove, and lighting on him" (Matt. 3:16). And later we are told "how God anointed Jesus of Nazareth with the Holy Spirit and power, and how he went around doing good and healing all who were under the power of the devil" (Acts 10:38). It was through the anointing that Jesus preached and healed the sick and cast out demons (Matt. 12:28). Through the anointing He offered Himself to God as an atonement for the sins of the world (Heb. 9:14). The anointing Spirit quickened Him from the dead (Romans 8:11). "If the Holy Son of God needed the anointing of the Spirit for His ministry, what supreme folly to imagine that we can dispense with it" (Nelson, 43). In Luke 4:18-19 Jesus Himself pointed out the Old Testament prophecy from Isaiah 61:1, 2: "The Spirit of the Sovereign Lord is on me, because the Lord has anointed me to preach good news to the poor. He has sent me to bind up the brokenhearted, to proclaim freedom for the captives and release for the prisoners, to proclaim the year of the Lord's favor and the day of vengeance of our God, to comfort all who mourn." Nelson says, "Anointed to preach, to heal, to liberate, to give sight, to proclaim the acceptable year of the Lord. What a ministry! And yet Jesus declared that our ministry was to be like His (42): John 14:12 states, "anyone who has faith in me will do what I have been doing." Such a ministry requires divine power, and anyone who expects to have a ministry for the Lord Jesus Christ needs all the power available. The fullness of the Holy Spirit is the only way we human beings can achieve any resemblance to our Lord Jesus Christ in any way.

2. **The Holy Spirit is our Advocate**. Jesus announced, "If you love me, you will obey what I command. And I will ask the Father, and he will give you another Counselor, to be with you forever—the Spirit of truth. The world cannot accept him, because it neither sees him nor knows him. But you know him, for he lives with you and will be in you" (John 14:15-17). This Advocate—or Comforter or Counselor—was to take the place of Jesus in the disciples' lives. In fact, the Advocate was to be more to them than Jesus had been. Jesus said that it was for the disciples' benefit that He go away and send the Advocate to them. The disciples could not receive the Spirit in fullness until Jesus had ascended: "It is for your good that I am going away. Unless I go away, the Counselor [Advocate] will not come to you; but if I go, I will send him to you" (John 16:7). Nelson states, "Amazing that the almighty Holy Spirit—should come down from the Father and make His abode in each believer, teaching, guiding, inspiring, helping us just at the moment, and in the way most needed" (44).

3. **Without the aid of the Holy Spirit we are spiritually inadequate**. We need the Holy Spirit to help us pray: "In the same way, the Spirit helps us in our weakness. We do not know what we ought to pray, but the Spirit himself intercedes for us with groans that words cannot express. And he who searches our hearts knows the mind of the Spirit, because the Spirit intercedes for the saints in accordance with God's will" (Rom. 8:26, 27). We need the Holy Spirit in order to be effective witnesses: "But you will receive power when the Holy Spirit comes on you; and you will be my witnesses in Jerusalem, and in all Judea and Samaria, and to the ends of the earth" (Acts 1:8). All Christians need the Holy Spirit to be able to bear fruit for Christ (John 15). The Holy Spirit makes Christ real to believers and allows Christ to be effective in their lives. "Christ dwelling in our hearts by faith through the mediation of the Holy Spirit will make our lives fruitful unto every good work and the fruit of the Spirit

will appear" (Nelson, 46).

4. **Without the Holy Spirit we cannot worship God acceptably**. Worship that is not inspired by the Holy Spirit is empty, mechanical, and meaningless. Without the Holy Spirit we cannot worship God as He deserves to be worshipped. Jesus said, "Yet a time is coming and has now come when the true worshipers will worship the Father in spirit and truth, for they are the kind of worshipers the Father seeks" (John 4:23). In fact Jesus adds to that statement by saying the Father is looking for anyone who will worship Him that way—in Spirit and in truth (v. 23). P. C. Nelson states,

   > How hard it is for hearts and lips untouched by the Holy Spirit to glorify Christ! How hollow it sounds! How offensive it must be to the ears of God! But when the Spirit comes in, a stream of praise and glory flows from our hearts and mouths; and while the Spirit sets Christ before our enchanted vision, we are transformed from one degree of glory to another by the Spirit of the Lord (2 Cor.3:18) (47).

5. **We cannot rightly interpret God's Word without the aid of "the Spirit of truth."** The Spirit alone can guide us into truth and teach us the way of God. Only the Holy Spirit can guide believers into all truth and teach the truth in all things: "But when he, the Spirit of truth, comes, he will guide you into all truth. He will not speak on his own; he will speak only what he hears, and he will tell you what is yet to come" (John 16:13). We have the Holy Scriptures today because the Holy Spirit inspired men to write the Word of God: "For prophecy never had its origin in the will of man, but men spoke from God as they were carried along by the Holy Spirit" (2 Peter 1:21). P. C. Nelson notes "How marvelous a privilege to have the very Spirit who inspired holy men of old to write the Word to look on the Sacred Page with us and help us understand its true spiritual meaning!" (47). Human

teachers can be of great help but only in so far as they have been taught by the Holy Spirit.

Robert C. Frost, in *Overflowing Life*, also points out that newly Spirit-filled believers will discover that the Word of God has suddenly become alive for them in a way they haven't experienced before. It is the purpose of the Holy Spirit to illuminate our understanding of God's Word (30). In fact, Frost comments, "The Word of God is the raw material the Holy Spirit uses to build Christ into our lives. As we live in the Word, the life of the Word becomes ours!" (30). Through the written Word, the Holy Spirit is able to make the Living Word real to us. "If we do not honor the place of the Holy Scriptures in our daily experience, we quickly grieve God's Spirit in us and frustrate His will for us. It is the deep desire of the Holy Spirit to make God's living Word our daily life. Jesus said, 'I am the bread of life.' May we quickly reply, 'Give us this day our daily bread'" (Frost, 32).

6. **The Spirit alone has power to lift us out of the self-life and place us into the Christ-life**. We gravitate downward to the level of the natural. The Spirit lifts us up to the supernatural. The Christianity of the New Testament is supernatural. If the Christianity in our churches today is not supernatural, if it is indeed too natural, then our churches are not following Christ. The Pentecostal movement is to call people away from the popularity of the world and into the supernatural manifestations of the New Testament church: "God also bearing them witness both with signs and wonders, and with divers miracles, and gifts of the Holy Ghost, according to his will" (Heb. 2:4).

7. **The Holy Spirit of God makes Jesus real to us in our personal experience** and then enables us to give evidence of our Lord to others. The Holy Spirit manifests God's life in us and through us in thought, word, and deed. Others "see" Christ in us as we demonstrate the fruit and gifts of the Spirit. To live is to witness! (Frost, 33). It is not a question of

> whether we are going to witness or not, but rather what we are going to be witnesses of. The Holy Spirit helps that witness to be effective. The purpose of the Holy Spirit in us is "that we may be a continual daily witness for Jesus Christ" (Frost, 33). The rules for witnessing are simple: Live Christ and love others. But even that simple rule is impossible without the Holy Spirit to express that love through us. Frost states, "There is no greater privilege given to man than sharing the Gifts of God's Son and His Spirit with others. . . . we pray that He will bring someone with a prepared and open heart across our path. May we be sensitive to God and others to recognize the encounter when it comes. God will divinely order our lives to reach others if we expectantly ask him to do so!" (34).

Obviously, most followers of Christ are able to worship and pray effectively, read the Scriptures accurately, and witness to others about the saving power of Christ. Not having received the baptism with the Holy Spirit doesn't mean that a believer is unable to serve Christ meaningfully. However, the baptism with the Holy Spirit brings a fullness, a new dimension of worship and prayer, and a fellowship with God that surpasses the Christian experience without the Holy Spirit Baptism. The Holy Spirit is our means of entering fully into an experience with God; therefore, receiving the baptism with the Holy Spirit allows us to transcend the human limitations in prayer and worship and also allows the fullness of the Holy Spirit to lead us into new depths of experience with our Lord.

In addition to the scriptural commands to be filled with the Holy Spirit, Ralph Riggs, in *The Spirit Himself*, offers some practical considerations to convince us that believers need to receive the baptism with the Holy Spirit. Riggs gives the following as a condensed list of many reasons:

1. God has provided it.
2. Jesus Himself received it.
3. Jesus commanded His disciples not to proceed without it.
4. All His disciples did receive it.
5. It brought about the conversion of 3,000 on the Day of

Pentecost.

6. It enabled the apostles to fill Jerusalem with their doctrine.
7. It enabled them to perform supernatural signs and wonders.
8. It enabled them to carry the Gospel to every creature of their generation (Col. 1:23).
9. It led the disciples' converts into the same kind of power (Acts 8:14, 15).
10. Christ commands all believers to be filled with the Spirit (Matt. 28:20, Eph. 5:18) (Riggs, 82-83).

Over and above this condensed list, though, Riggs offers other specific and biblically supported reasons for considering the Baptism with the Holy Spirit as essential for all Christians.

1. The baptism with the Holy Spirit "marks the coming of the Holy Spirit into one's life as a Person in His own name and right" (Riggs, 79). The Holy Spirit comes at conversion primarily to witness of Christ and with the purpose of making Christ real to the new believer. However, at the Baptism with the Holy Spirit, He comes in and fills the waiting believer—a new relationship with the third person of the trinity.
2. The baptism with the Holy Spirit is the "fulfillment of the promise of the Father which endues men with power from on high" (Luke 24:49). As glorious as was the message of salvation, the disciples were not even to think about leaving Jerusalem or think about preaching one sermon until they had received this power to preach and to testify: "You will receive power after the Holy Spirit comes upon you" (Acts. 1:8). Power first and then witnessing.
3. The baptism with the Holy Spirit establishes a relationship with Christians' new head and leader (Riggs, 81). The Holy Spirit is and was meant to be the Personal Head and Leader and Commander of the Church. How can we function without our God-appointed leader? We receive the fullness of the Holy Spirit only through baptism.
4. The baptism with the Holy Spirit is our divine equipment. Eph. 6:11 tells us to "Put on the full armor of God so that

> you can take your stand against the devil's schemes." Why neglect this splendid, effective equipment which God has provided? (Riggs, 82)

We cannot be effective witnesses for God without the power of the Spirit—"But you will receive power when the Holy Spirit comes on you; and you will be my witnesses in Jerusalem, and in all Judea and Samaria, and to the ends of the earth" (Acts 1:8). We cannot bear fruit without Christ (John 15), and it is the Holy Spirit who makes Christ real to us and allows the work of Christ to be effective in our lives.

The baptism with the Holy Spirit is not something we can take or leave as we choose. It is very important that we receive this experience and have it working for and in us. The baptism with the Holy Spirit is indeed more than a spiritual luxury—it is a necessity and should be sought with great earnestness by every child of God (Nelson, 48).

Along with the reasons from Scripture for receiving the baptism with the Holy Spirit, Rufus Moseley in a pamphlet titled "The Gift of the Holy Spirit" offers some practical reasons in the language of everyday common sense to convince us that we do indeed need the infilling baptism with the Holy Spirit (qtd. Jorstad, 61-63):

1. It is only through this heavenly gift empowering us, guiding us, transforming us that we have immediate union with the glorified Jesus and are given power to do His work and His will and to grow up into His likeness.
2. If Jesus had remained on earth, with all His power to heal and perform miracles, He still would be in only one place at a time; He could not be with everyone at one time since He would be limited by a physical body. Since He went to heaven, He shared this power with all His disciples—giving them power to minister, and knowledge so they would know what to do and what to say to further His kingdom.
3. When Jesus hung on the cross of shame and agony, He gave up the Holy Breath or Holy Ghost; when we receive the Holy Spirit, we are filled with the Holy breath of God.
4. The Holy Spirit knows Jesus and can reveal Him as He is.

Humans tend to carve Jesus down into their own abilities, but the Holy Spirit changes us to fit a more heavenly mold.

5. The Holy Spirit, in revealing Jesus to us, also reveals ourselves to us. We are convicted of sin and weakness by seeing Jesus' sinless-ness and perfection. As we see our sin, He brings us to repentance and forgiveness.
6. The Holy Spirit guides us into all truth (John 16:13).
7. Through submission to the Holy Spirit, the body becomes consciously the Lord's.

The urgent priority of receiving the fullness of the Holy Spirit baptism was stressed by Jesus Himself. His last command to His disciples was to wait until they had received the power from above—the gift of the Father (Acts 1:8). Only then would they be dynamic Christians equipped to deliver the good news of God's love to mankind. Human power is unable to accomplish the task, but human beings endowed with power from on high could turn the world upside down. That power came at Pentecost (Durasoff, 9).

CHAPTER X

RESULTS OF RECEIVING THE BAPTISM WITH THE HOLY SPIRIT

We will get a clearer and fuller view of what the baptism with the Holy Spirit is if we will notice what this baptism does. Acts 1:8 states concisely "You will receive power, after the Holy Spirit is come upon you; and you will be witnesses . . . ." The baptism with the Holy Spirit, then, imparts power—power for service (Torrey, *Baptism,* 20). This power is not identical for each person; in fact each individual may see it manifested differently. The passage in I Cor. 12:4, 8, 11 (ASV) clarifies thus:

> There are different kinds of gifts, but the same Spirit. . . . Now to each one the manifestation of the Spirit is given for the common good. To one there is given through the Spirit the message of wisdom, to another the message of knowledge by means of the same Spirit, to another faith by the same Spirit, to another gifts of healing by that one Spirit . . . to another the ability to speak in different kinds of tongues . . . . All these are the work of one and the same Spirit, and he gives them to each man just as **he determines.**

John F. Walvoord and others give at least ten results of the infilling one receives from the Baptism with the Holy Spirit. He gives the following as evidence of a Spirit baptized life.

1. Progressive Sanctification—Christians controlled by the Spirit and empowered to live the life of God will manifest a change in character. The former sin nature is still present, but it has been reckoned dead and the new nature of the Spirit is producing the fruit of the Spirit. Galatians 5:22-23 tells us the infilling of the Spirit will produce fruit in Christians' lives: "But the fruit of the Spirit is love, joy, peace, long-suffering, kindness, goodness, faithfulness, meekness, self-control; against such there is no law" (Walvoord, 219). A Christian's sanctification does not result from self-effort or from the will of natural man. Sanctification is a product of the Holy Spirit in a yielded life. True Christian character cannot be produced apart from the work of the Holy Spirit. The Spirit of God promises that with the filling of the Spirit the longings of man's nature for a holy life in the will of God may be satisfied (Walvoord, 220).

The Holy Spirit made a new beginning in our century, calling humble and hungry souls to Himself. Those who would cry for revival of the supernatural and spiritual work of God gave God a chance to work in and through His people. This Pentecostal movement of the 20th century is made up of people of all nations and cultures who believe that signs will follow faith and that divine manifestations should not be denied the church of our day. The church now is confirmed by divine manifestations just as the confirmations in the early church: "God also bearing them witness both with signs and wonders, and with divers miracles, and gifts of the Holy Ghost, according to his will" (Heb. 2:4).

2. Teaching—Christ predicted the teaching ministry of the Holy Spirit for the apostles: "But when he, the Spirit of truth, comes, he will guide you into all truth" (John 16:13). The teaching ministry is extended to all Christians. The work of the Holy Spirit in teaching is multiple. The Word of God is written by inspiration of the Holy Spirit, and its divine author, the Spirit of truth, is its best teacher. Christ realized the limitations of the disciples in learning all He would teach them, so Christ told them, "I have yet many things to say unto you, but you cannot bear them now. Howbeit when he, the Spirit of truth, is come, he shall guide you into all the truth: for he shall not speak from himself; but what things soever he shall hear, these shall he speak: and he shall declare unto you the things that are to come" (John 16:12-13). The disciples were in no position to learn about the cross, the resurrection, nor the ascension until after these events had occurred. The Spirit of God, then, had to be the chief agent in teaching them. Still today the Spirit sometimes reveals deep spiritual truths that can be understood only by those spiritually qualified to be taught by the Spirit (Walvoord, 220). Carnality will keep Christians from hearing those teachings of the Spirit. The Spirit also warns against error, and the anointing (indwelling) of the Spirit allows Christians to be taught the truth of God even without human teachers (Walvoord, 221)

3. Guidance—Guidance is essential to a life in the will of God. Guidance is similar to teaching but is distinctive in character. Guidance is the application of the truths made clear by the teaching ministry of the Holy Spirit. Guidance is the application of general Biblical principles to particular problems at hand. The Spirit of God provides necessary guidance for the many details of each life, including the call of an individual to an appointed field of service. Guidance is given to those walking in the will of God; surrender to God is necessary: "that you may prove what is the good and acceptable and perfect will of God" (Romans 12:1-2). Guidance becomes the personal direction of the life in the will of God (Walvoord, 221). Guidance is an essential part of God's provision for the Christian: "For as many as are led by the Spirit of God, these are the sons of God" (Romans 8:14).

Believers sometimes worry that they won't know the guidance of the Spirit when it comes. They sometimes have difficulty distinguishing between their own desires and the voice of the Spirit and therefore wonder if they are listening to themselves or to the Spirit. The key is in keeping in such close communication with the Holy Spirit that His voice can be recognized. Mark A. Barclift, in "Supernatural Guidance in Acts 16:6-10," states that as "long as a believer is attempting to follow the leading of the Holy Spirit, the Spirit is perfectly capable of keeping that person on course" (10).

4. Assurance—Assurance of salvation depends upon a proper understanding of revelation and of the witness of the Spirit. Some

Christians do not have assurance of salvation because they fail to meet the conditions for the filling of the Spirit and the resulting ministry of the Spirit to their hearts. The Spirit bears witness that God is ours and we belong to Him. Romans 8:16 states, "The Spirit himself testifies with our Spirit that we are God's children." We see the same concept in Gal. 4:6—"Because you are sons, God sent the Spirit of his Son into our hearts, the Spirit who calls out, Abba, Father" (see also I John 3:24; 4:13). Again, it is carnality in the life that will rob a Christian of the assurance of belonging to God.

5. Worship—Sometimes Christians associate worship with ritual, public worship, houses of worship. In Scripture, however, worship is the adoration of God by those who know Him (Walvoord, 222). Ephesians 5:18-20 reports that immediately after the command to be filled with the Spirit, there is mention of praise and thanksgiving both of which result from a life lived in fellowship with God. As the Holy Spirit produces love, joy, peace, assurance in the lives of Christians, they cannot help but perceive God's blessings and praise the God who provides those blessings. Walvoord believes that "true worship in the fullest sense of the word is possible only for those who are filled with the Spirit" (222).

6. Prayer—The prayer life of a believer is inseparable from the spiritual life. The prayer life will prosper in proportion to the spiritual life of the believer. For example, the teaching ministry of the Spirit tells of the many promises in God's Word. The guidance of the Spirit provides intelligent prayer, asking for the revealed will of God. Sanctification allows believers to pray with faith and power. Praise and thanksgiving allow the Spirit to direct the prayer life. The Holy Spirit leads believers into intercession: "In like manner the Spirit also helps our infirmity: for we know not how to pray as we ought; but the Spirit himself makes intercession for us with groanings which cannot be uttered" (Romans 8:26). When we are unable to pray, the Spirit prays through us. The Holy Spirit is inseparable from any vital prayer life (Walvoord, 223).

It is by praying in the Spirit that we are strengthened to overcome obstacles in our daily walk, to defeat the enemy in spiritual warfare, and to succeed in walking daily with Christ. For many believers, praying in the Spirit means victoriously facing martyrdom and persecution. For some, praying in the Spirit enables them to simply keep up the pace in their ministry or work as they continue reaching out to people. And for others it may mean the difference between overcoming or succumbing to personal struggles. But the greatest effect of praying in the Spirit may be on the lives of other people. We do not know for whom or for what we are praying when we speak in tongues. God uses us mightily for overcoming evil and for the pulling down of strongholds in the spiritual realm. Sometimes we see the results and sometimes we do not see the results. However, praying in the Spirit has tremendous power whether we see the results or not.

If we are filled with God's Spirit, declares Robert Frost, we are filled with "never-failing prayer!" (*Overflowing*, 18). Frost gives an example of a pastor who exclaimed right after receiving the fullness of God's Spirit, "Why, prayer won't be a chore anymore!" (18). And of course, the pastor was right. The Holy Spirit desires to fill our lives with prayer and praise.

Usually, praying in the Spirit is the gateway to ministering in all the gifts of the Spirit because that kind of prayer helps us to hear what God is saying and how He is directing us by His Spirit. There have been cases, however, in which Spirit led believers have been known to operate in the spiritual gifts although they have not spoken in tongues. Nevertheless, without the Holy Spirit we cannot operate in His gifts.

7. Service—All service for God is dependent upon the power of God for its fruitfulness. The power of the Spirit was revealed by Christ Himself: "'Whoever believes in me, as the Scripture has said, streams of living water will flow from within him.' By this he meant the Spirit, whom those who believed in him were later to receive" (John 7:38-39). Natural man is insufficient for service to God. The spring of all blessing must be unhindered in its flow—and this condition exists only when the believer is filled with the Holy Spirit.

Service and sanctification, knowledge of the Word of God, "guidance, assurance, worship, and prayer life are not separate elements which can fall into separate categories, but they are all varied lights of all the colors of the spiritual life, which combined form a holy life in the will of God" (Walvoord, 224). The theories of self-development or self-achievement are in direct contradiction with the Scriptural doctrine which points to the indwelling Spirit as the source of fruitfulness of any Christian's life.

While agreeing that the Baptism with the Holy Spirit is primarily for the purpose of empowering for service, R. A. Torrey still states we need to remember that the Baptism is accompanied by a great moral uplift (20). Acts 2:47 tells us that the newly baptized communed together, "praising God and enjoying the favor of all the people," and in Acts 4:33 those who had recently been "filled with the Holy Spirit" (Acts 4:31) are described thus: "much grace was with them all."

8. Faith—The Holy Spirit of Faith makes faith more real to us and more a part of our lives, just as He makes Christ more real to us and more a part of our lives. Frost gives an example of the Holy Spirit and Faith:

> A professional colleague of mine has just recently been filled with the Holy Spirit. A brush fire was threatening the home of a mutual friend early one Sunday afternoon. An appeal for prayer was made, and we all responded by seeking God's protection for their home. The flames were checked and their home was saved. My colleague later told us of their prayer experience at the time. They had taken time out from the activities of Sunday dinner and had prayed an earnest but short prayer for God's intervention. He immediately felt that God had heard and would act accordingly. They rejoiced but were not surprised to learn of the outcome. 'It's a funny thing,' he said, 'but before being filled with God's Spirit, I never would have had that kind of faith' (*Overflowing*, 19).

9. Joy—God brings a new joy into our hearts when we are filled with the Holy Spirit. Praise is spontaneous. The Holy Spirit has a way of linking our hearts with Christ when we praise Him. To know the touch of Jesus and His joy is to be spoiled for anything else that this world calls joy (Frost, *Overflowing*, 20). Real joy cannot be experienced apart from the Holy Spirit. "And the disciples were filled with joy, and with the Holy Spirit" (Acts 13:52); and "May the God of hope fill you with all joy and peace as you trust in him, so that you may overflow with hope by the power of the Holy Spirit" (Romans 15:13).

Father Edward O'Connor, in *Ave Maria* magazine, reported this: "Whatever other particular effects may have occurred, peace and joy seem to have been received by all, . . . of those who have been touched by the Spirit" (quoted in Ranaghan, 133).

10. Love—One of the most amazing characteristics of the latter day outpouring of the Holy Spirit is the bond of love seen between real Spirit-filled believers. The Spirit cuts across all boundaries of doctrine, theology, and denomination, and through race or economic status. The Holy Spirit mixes everyone together in His love when we allow Him to harmonize us in the will of God. All denominations are able to join together to pray, sing, worship, and work together for Jesus because the Holy Spirit unifies the body of Christ with His love. Frost says, "Man-made fences cannot hold back the rising tide of God's Spirit!" (*Overflowing*, 40). One purpose for the Holy Spirit on earth is to unify and perfect Christ's Body, the Living Church (Frost, 41).

Psalm 133 states, "Behold, how good and how pleasant it is for brethren to dwell together in unity! It is like the precious ointment upon the head, that ran down upon the beard, even Aaron's beard: that went down to the skirts of his garments . . . "(vv. 1-2). Oil is a type of the Holy Spirit. "It speaks of spiritual healing and personal consecration. Zion represents God's chosen people. The morning dew symbolizes the promises and freshness of life which envelop the lives of God's people baptized by His Spirit" (Frost, *Overflowing,* 41). Christ, too, like Aaron, received the anointing oil of consecration from His Father. The oil was abundant, not only for His head, but descending in a mighty outpouring on the many members of His earthly body (Acts 2:33).

When a believer receives the Baptism with the Holy Spirit, it is a personal devotional experience of the deepest kind (Richard W. Bishop, 10). The newly filled person will usually have a greater awareness of a personal and present God. Dennis Bennett, author of

Nine O'Clock in the Morning, described his experience with expressions such as these:

> I became more and more aware of God in me . . . The presence of God . . . enveloped me. . . . Never had I experienced God's presence in such reality as now (23, 24).

Graham Pulkingham, pastor of the Episcopal Church of the Redeemer in Houston, gives a somewhat similar description of the effect of receiving the Baptism with the Holy Spirit:

> Rather soon after I knelt, all awareness of the men and their prayers, of the room and even of myself was obliterated by the immense presence of God's power. He was unmistakably there . . . .
> In a moment of breathless adoration, all my longing for love was satisfied and my inner being was swept clean of defilement from the tip of my toes to the top of my head as with a mighty rush of wind. (75, 76).

Many others testify to the same kinds of experience—to a more intimate relationship with God after being baptized with the Spirit. They became more aware of His love for them, and they in turn have a greater love for and devotion to Him (Bishop, 11).

Far from considering the initial experience of receiving the Baptism with the Holy Spirit as an end in itself, most of those who receive realize that it is only a beginning into the deeper, more joyful, more victorious life of the believer in the Spirit. Only through such Holy Spirit infilling can believers become the channels through which the Holy Spirit can flow in bringing blessing to others and to their risen Lord (Bishop, 13).

Bishop offers other noticeable results of the infilling baptism with the Holy Spirit (17-21):

- People wanted to pray and spend time in Church
- They tried to exclude worldliness from their lives
- They prayed for cleansing and consecration more than ever before
- They acknowledged the reign of Christ in their souls

- Baptism involved a growing relationship with God
- Restitution and heart searching became common
- It made people happy and free
- They became more committed to evangelism
- They understood the infilling to be empowerment for service
- What the empowered person *was* was at least as important as what he *did*
- The empowered person was to die to self and let Christ reign fully within
- Spirit-baptism altered priorities

When the Holy Spirit encounters a person, that person's life is dramatically changed—the trajectory of his life is changed. For example, a Christ-persecuting Saul becomes a Christ-preaching Paul. Cringing disciples become bold ambassadors of their Lord (Bishop, 9).

The apostle Paul promises wonderful things for those who walk in the Life of the Holy Spirit. He claims it is a life without condemnation (Rom. 8:1), a life of assurance and confident approach to God (Rom. 8:15, 16), and a life where human limitations are compensated for by the power of the Holy Spirit (Rom. 8:26, 27). He also, though, describes the power of the Spirit-filled life when he says "We are hard pressed on every side, but not crushed; perplexed, but not in despair; persecuted, but not abandoned; struck down, but not destroyed" (II Cor. 4:8-9). The Holy Spirit provides the power when and where and how we most need it.

CHAPTER XI

HOW TO RECEIVE THE BAPTISM WITH THE HOLY SPIRIT

How does one receive the Baptism with the Holy Spirit? Is there a formula one must follow? Are there options or different formats one can practice? After having seen that the Baptism with the Holy Spirit is distinct from conversion, that it is desirable for all believers, and that it is available for Christians today, then we are ready to discover how to receive this blessing.

Some believe that only through the imposition of Apostolic hands could the Spirit be given. Many commentators (some listed above in Chapter IV) assume that Philip could not bestow the gift of the Spirit on his converts because he was not an apostle. The incident in Samaria is the one in question. Philip had faithfully preached Christ as the Savior and Healer to many. His listeners had received the message, had been saved, healed, baptized in water. Now they were ready for the Holy Spirit baptism. Here, then, come the apostles, Peter and John, who saw that these believers were ready for the next step, instructed them, laid their hands on them, and the people were filled with the Spirit just as those at Pentecost had been.

This incident is not sufficient to show that Philip could not have been the instrument by which the people received the Holy Spirit, points out P. C. Nelson, because such an assumption ignores ten very important facts.

1. Scripture nowhere states that the giving of the Spirit is an

apostolic function only.

2. If such had been the case, at Pentecost the apostles should have been filled with the Spirit themselves, then laid hands on the others to receive. But all received at the same time.
3. There is no record that the apostles laid hands on the 3000 that received the Spirit on repentance (Acts 2:38, 39).
4. Cornelius and his friends were filled with the Spirit before Peter had a chance to lay hands on them (there is no command that Peter lay hands on them before they received).
5. Ananias was not an apostle, yet he laid hands on Paul at Damascus and Paul was filled with the Spirit.
6. Peter stated at Pentecost that the promise was to "you and to your children, and to all that are afar off, even as many as the Lord our God shall call." This promise could not have been fulfilled if apostolic hands were necessary before each baptism.
7. On this theory assemblies established without the presence of an apostle could not have received the Baptism with the Holy Spirit.
8. The Spirit could not have been given to anyone after the death of the last apostle. The history of the church proves that the same manifestations of the Spirit were in evidence long after the last apostle had passed away.
9. The Scriptures do not indicate that it was God's plan to withhold the Spirit from believers during the dispensation of Grace—"By this he meant the Spirit, whom those who believed in him were later to receive" (John 7:39).
10. The gift of the Spirit could not have been renewed unless the apostles were brought back; however, during the early years of the 20th century there was a new outpouring in Topeka, Houston, and Los Angeles, even in all parts of the world. The experience was renewed with New Testament evidences, "and we are witnesses of these things and so is the Holy Spirit, whom God hath given to them that obey him" (Acts 5:32) (Nelson, 23-25).

Pentecostals speak of "baptism in the Spirit" rather than "with the Spirit" (Stott, 25). The Greek preposition may be translated either way. "The expression chosen," says Stott, "is likely to depend on whether one considers that water-baptism should be administered by immersion or by affusion. Those who practice immersion speak of baptism in the Spirit presumably because they think of the Spirit as the element in which one is plunged. Since it is when the Holy Spirit is 'poured out' upon people that they are said to be 'baptized,' however, 'baptism with the Spirit' is preferable" (25).

Ralph Riggs, in his book *The Spirit Himself*, offers a few simple steps which will prepare us for receiving the baptism with the Holy Spirit (101-105).

1. We must first be saved. It is impossible for a sinner to receive the Baptism with the Spirit. John 14:16, 17 reads, "I will ask the Father, and he will give you another Counselor to be with you forever—the Spirit of truth. *The world cannot accept him*, because it neither sees him nor knows him" (italics added). The Holy Spirit cannot come into an unclean person; He can come only into a person who has been yielded to Him. A definite born-again experience is preparation for receiving the Baptism with the Holy Spirit. Ralph Riggs states, "The blood is first applied, and then the oil" (102).
2. We must obey. Acts 5:32 states, "We are witnesses of these things, and so is the Holy Spirit, whom God has *given to those who obey him*" (italics added). If there is any measure of rebellion against God, that rebellion will have to be surrendered to Him. We are commanded in Eph. 5:18 to "be filled with the Spirit." Can we be obedient to God and disobey that command?
3. We must ask. Luke 11:13 declares, "If you then, though you are evil, know how to give good gifts to your children, how much more will your Father in heaven *give the Holy Spirit to those who ask him*?" (italics added). God is able to give the Holy Spirit to all who ask, and He is willing to give the Holy Spirit to all who ask. But in fact He gives the Holy Spirit only to those who ask. James 4:2 says, "You have not because you ask not."

4. We must believe. Gal. 3:14 tells us that "he redeemed us . . . so that *by faith we might receive* the promise of the Spirit" (italics added). This experience is called the "gift of the Holy Spirit." Gifts are not earned or won by merit or by hard work. Gifts cannot be forced from the giver. The Holy Spirit is a God-sent gift, and we receive Him by faith alone. He has promised, and "Faith is the hand that reaches out and receives the gift of the Holy Spirit" (Riggs, 108).

L. Thomas Holdcroft, in his article "Receiving the Baptism in the Holy Spirit," gives similar advice for receiving the baptism of the Holy Spirit. But since the order is different and since he adds two additional criteria, sharing his list seems warranted (4-7).

1. Repentance. "Then Peter said to them, 'Repent and be baptized every one of you . . . and you will receive the gift of the Holy Spirit" (Acts 2:38). The Spirit baptizes no one without that person's consent. Repentance is an important evidence of that consent to be filled. Repentance involves a change of mind. Water baptism often is an outward sign of an inward change of mind—from the old way to God's way. Water baptism is not a condition for receiving Spirit baptism, but the change of heart that motivates water baptism may also prepare one to receive the Baptism with the Holy Spirit.
2. Faith. Galatians 3:14 says, " . . .that we might receive the promise of the Spirit through faith." Faith is the process by which believers receive the Spirit. It is not earning or deserving the Spirit. It is simply receiving Him by faith. For the Christian, the object of faith is always Jesus Christ; when the believer receives Spirit baptism, Christ is received as the divine baptizer.
3. Obedience. Acts 5:32 states, ". . . the Holy Ghost, whom God hath given to them that obey him." Obedience includes following Christ in externals such as water baptism. It also includes internal attitudes of the heart and submissive obedience to God. When one totally submits his heart, then he is obedient. Verla A. Mooth writes, "When the self-life expires, the fullness of the Spirit comes in as naturally as air rushes

into a vacuum. . . . This 'death of self' is a gateway to the Spirit-filled life" (49, quoted in Holdcroft, 5).

4. Personal Purity. The apostle Paul emphasized that defiling sin or worldliness is not compatible with the indwelling of the Spirit of God. "Don't you know that you yourselves are God's temple and that God's Spirit lives in you? If anyone destroys God's temple, God will destroy him; for God's temple is sacred, and you are that temple" (I Cor. 3:16-17). It has been well said, "God does not require golden vessels, neither does He seek for silver ones, but He must have clean ones" (Holdcroft, 6).
5. Wholehearted Desire. One expresses desire by asking. Jesus taught that the Father in heaven would "give the Holy Spirit to those who ask him" (Luke 11:13). Jesus also "stood and said in a loud voice, 'If a man is thirsty, let him come to me and drink. Whoever believes in me, streams of living water will flow from within him.' By this he meant the Spirit, whom those who believed in him were later to receive" (John 7:37-39). The original 120 on the Day of Pentecost were in prayer and supplication while they waited for the promised empowerment from on high; their willingness to wait for the promise shows their wholehearted desire (Holdcroft, 6).
6. Praise. The disciples were continually in a spirit of praise (Luke 24:35) before they received the Spirit. The same is true of those who received at the house of Cornelius and of others in Acts and the Epistles. The outpouring of the Holy Spirit seems "clearly related to an audible verbal expression of praise to God" (Holdcroft, 6-7).

Arthur H. Graves points out that there is no mystery about receiving the Baptism with the Holy Spirit. "We receive the baptism in the Spirit," says Graves, "just as we receive other things from God" (12). The word "receive" is the key. John uses the same word in speaking of Christ—"Yet to all who received him, to those who believed in his name he gave the right to become children of God" (John 1:12). Paul used the same word when he says, "we also rejoice in God through our Lord Jesus Christ, through whom we have now received reconciliation" (Rom. 5:11). And, Graves adds, in the last chapter of Revelation we see the same word when we read, "Whoever is thirsty, let him come; and whoever wishes, let him take [same word used of receiving the Spirit] the water of life freely" (Rev. 22:17). If we know how to receive Christ, then we also know how to receive the baptism with the Holy Spirit (12).

Samuel Chadwick, in "The Way to Pentecost," states "The Spirit-filled must be Spirit-ruled. This extraordinary gift is for ordinary people. All may be filled as full and as truly as the 120 on the Day of Pentecost. The conditions are the same for all: Repent, ask, receive, obey" (30). The work of baptizing believers with the Holy Spirit is God's work, not man's work. G. R. Carlson stresses the fact that the Bible does not emphasize how we should receive, but "how God will give. 'He will give . . . He will send . . . He will pour out . . . He will baptize'" (24).

The clear instructions come from biblical examples. Peter told his hearers to "repent" (Acts 2:38). Sin must be confessed. God gives the Holy Spirit to "them that obey him" (Acts 5:32). Faith is the condition by which God gives all His gifts to believers—salvation, sanctification, healing, the gifts of the Spirit, and in the same manner also the Baptism with the Holy Spirit (John 7:39). Though it may sound overly simple, we must remember to "take" the gift God offers. Revelation 22:17 states, "And whosoever will, let him take the water of life freely." The same word used for "take" is translated "receive" in the passages relating to receiving the Holy Spirit (Carlson, 24).

David du Plessis adds that we cannot pray or praise ourselves into this experience with God. He adds, "You surrender to Christ and He gives you the experience. But keep your mind on Christ (II Cor. 10:5, 6) while you wait for the experience" (71). He also believes that as surely as one can feel the effect of the water on the body in water baptism, so certainly can one feel the effect of the Holy Spirit within the body (71). There are many possible effects of receiving (some shake, some tremble, some feel a deep stirring inside, some cry, some shout, some laugh, and some just grow silent for a few minutes). But the one thing that you can expect, according to Pentecostal tradition and the Scriptures, is speaking in tongues. It happened every time according to Acts 2:4, Acts 10:44-46, and Acts 19:6. As the language of the Holy Spirit flows from your lips, Du Plessis adds, you will discover the truth of II Tim. 1:7: you will have received the Spirit of "power, of love, and of a sound mind." Newly filled believers may have tears trickling over their cheeks, but those emotions will be deep and sacred and those same people will have sound minds—will not act crazy (Du Plessis, 73) but will glorify God with new tongues understood by God Himself.

Guy P. D. Duffield and Nathaniel Van Cleave report the most common ways that those in the early Church received the Holy Spirit (319-320). The variety is interesting:

1. Suddenly, while sitting and expecting Him to come (Acts 2:1-4)
2. Instantly and unexpectedly, while listening to a sermon (Acts 10:44-46)
3. Through prayer and the laying on of the apostles' hands (Acts 8:14-17, 9:17, 19:6)
4. Through the seeker's personal prayer and faith (Luke 11:9-13, John 7:37-39).

True, the apostles prayed for believers to manifest the Holy Spirit by speaking in tongues through the laying on of hands. For example, when Peter and John came to Samaria to visit the new believers there, "Peter and John placed their hands on them and they received the Holy Spirit" (Acts 8:17). Again in Acts 19:6 the new believers in Ephesus received the Holy Spirit when hands were placed on them. This is a Biblical model. And we have seen God fill thousands of people in this manner because He continues to work this way. Many people who receive their prayer language receive it through the laying on of hands, or through the direct sovereign will of God. However, there are numerous accounts in which the Holy Spirit has come privately upon individuals who have begun to speak in tongues without the laying on the hands. We cannot limit God.

Many people ask about the importance of laying on of hands. They wonder, "What is the role of laying on of hands in the process of the Baptism with the Holy Spirit?" The practice of laying on of hands was given a new meaning and effect by the Church. In the Old Testament the rite was used with

1. The offering of sacrifice (Lev. 1:3ff),
2. The consecration of Levites (Num. 8:10), and
3. The imparting of a blessing (Gen. 48:14).

In the New Testament the laying on of hands is used in connection with

1. Healing (Mark 5:23, 7:32, 8:23-25, Acts 9:12-17, 28:8)
2. Baptizing (Acts 8:17-19, 19:5ff, and perhaps Heb. 6:2)
3. The distribution of functions or offices in the Church (Acts 6:6, 13:3, I Tim. 4:14, II Tim. 1:6) (Ranaghan, 85).

As a gesture of ritual, then, it may have more than one meaning or significance depending on the situation. When connected with the Baptism with the Holy Spirit, it was used in the apostolic church in baptismal initiation. It was used with or to complete the baptismal process, according to Ranaghan, especially Peter and John in Samaria, or Ananias with Paul. But it was not a necessary function or act for people to receive the Baptism with the Holy Spirit, for example with Cornelius and friends or at the Day of Pentecost. It may be part of the process of receiving, but is certainly not necessary to receiving the Baptism with the Holy Spirit (85).

Group prayer, or praying with someone to receive the Holy Spirit, is often accompanied with laying hands on the head or shoulders of the one being prayed for. Paul used the same practice in the New Testament. For example when Paul exhorts Timothy not to neglect the gift given to him, notice that Paul reminds Timothy that he received the gift "through a prophetic message when the body of elders laid their hands on you" (I Tim. 4:14). And again in II Timothy 1:6 Paul reminds Timothy to use the gift "which is in you through the laying on of hands." Many consider this gift to be the Baptism with the Holy Spirit. The same practice of laying hands on a seeker is used today. Ranaghan reports that the early Protestant Pentecostals of 1901 took a daring step in laying hands on those to receive. "They did it in simple imitation of the New Testament scenes which depicted an outpouring of the Spirit. They saw it as an instrument used by God for this purpose" (103).

Although not a necessary part of the Baptism with the Holy Spirit, laying on of hands is a common practice for several reasons:

1. It is a spontaneous gesture of reaching out; it's found in religions throughout the world.
2. It is a sign of mutual concern; it binds those praying with the one being prayed for.
3. It is prayer in action, a corporeal manifestation and embodiment of prayer. Man often needs such physical connections in encounters with the God of Spirit.
4. It has proved helpful in encouraging a deeper faith-life, especially in gifts and fruit of the Spirit (Ranaghan, 104).

The terms used to describe the way the Holy Spirit comes on believers all seem to show that the experience comes from God—not anything of our own work. God "pours out" or "sheds forth" His Spirit. He "baptizes" or "fills" and "gives the gift of the Spirit" which "fell" on men—obviously the experience did not originate with them. Acts 11:17 states "God gave them the gift" and again that they were to "receive the gift" (Acts 2:38). There is no way that man can earn or merit the Baptism with the Holy Spirit. It is the gift of God. However, says Frank Rice, the term "receive" implies "taking the gift in contrast to having it offered. Therefore the believer should not imagine that he can do nothing to receive. He does not wait passively for the magic moment to arrive. Having submitted himself to God's sovereign will for himself, he by faith must take—receive—the Holy Spirit" (10).

CHAPTER XII

AFTER RECEIVING THE BAPTISM WITH THE HOLY SPIRIT

Almost everyone who ever surrendered to Christ can remember the attempts which Satan made to stop the decision to follow Christ. We don't really feel much opposition from the enemy until we take steps to make a new, deeper commitment to Christ. The same opposition will come when we make a decision to move into the overcoming life of walking with the Holy Spirit. We can choose to live on the borderline of our Christian experience or we can choose to go on into a Spirit-filled life with Christ. And the same Bible that says "you must be born again," says "Be filled with the Spirit."

Jesus told the disciples, "you will receive power when the Holy Spirit comes upon you" (Acts 1:5). The devil does not want to see a powerful church or powerful people witnessing for Christ. Consequently, he constantly attacks the message of the Baptism with the Holy Spirit. God's answer to people's need for power is the Baptism with the Holy Spirit. The scriptures have many calls to repentance and many places describing the plan of salvation. But the Epistles contain an equal proportion of scripture commanding every believer to be filled with the Holy Spirit and to walk in the Spirit in a life of fruitful service.

Sometimes after having received the Baptism with the Holy Spirit as confirmed by speaking in tongues, people need to know what praying in the Spirit will do for them. Here are some ideas that can result in a more powerful spiritual life.

First, it is important to pray in the Spirit daily. Praying in the Spirit fortifies an individual mentally, spiritually, and emotionally at all times. The Holy Spirit will not leave us nor forsake us. People can pray in the Spirit or with the mind at any time—silently or aloud. If something seems to be lacking when praying in the Spirit, it is important to continue. We walk by faith and not by feeling. As we continue praying in the Spirit a sense of fluency will grow through time. Only as one prays often does one become fluent in prayer—whether the prayer is in the language of the Holy Spirit or the language of man.

Second, doubts may arise about our experience in the Baptism with the Holy Spirit and spiritual conflict may set in. The spiritual conflict we must be prepared for is not simple. There will be spiritual conflict against the world: we are told "Do not love the world or anything in the world. If anyone loves the world, the love of the Father is not in him. For everything in the world—the cravings of sinful man, the lust of his eyes and the boasting of what he has and does—comes not from the Father but from the world. The world and its desires pass away, but the man who does the will of God lives forever" (I John 2:15-17). Then there will also be spiritual conflict against the flesh: we are told "live by the Spirit, and you will not gratify the desires of the sinful nature. For the sinful nature desires what is contrary to the Spirit" (Gal. 5:16-17). And additionally there will be spiritual conflict against the wicked devil himself (Bright, 44-45): we are told "Your enemy the devil prowls around like a roaring lion looking for someone to devour. Resist him, standing firm in the faith" (I Peter 5:8-9). However, we also know that the power within us is stronger than the power in the whole world, all the flesh, and the devil himself all combined. Being baptized with the Holy Spirit gives us that power we need to overcome evil and follow our Lord.

Charles W. Ford, in "Walking in the Spirit," reminds us that when the mind and actions are under the control of the Holy Spirit, then Christians can be said to be "walking in the Spirit" (20). Temptations to yield to the sins of the flesh will always be with the believer, but those temptations should not control him. Walking in the Spirit is not some mystical experience above the reach of the ordinary Christian. It should be a normal pattern of living for all believers (20). The Word of God gives instruction as to what believers can do to resist the temptations of the flesh and be led by the Holy Spirit. Romans 8:13 tells us "If by the Spirit you put to death the misdeeds of the body, you will live." Romans chapters 6 and 8 state clearly that the Holy Spirit helps believers in this conflict with temptations of the flesh. Victory is possible through the power of the Holy Spirit (21). "Yielding and responding to the Spirit makes the difference between victory and defeat, between walking in the flesh and walking in the Spirit" (21).

George Holmes tells how under the influence of a saintly mariner he was led into the experience of the Spirit's indwelling. Shortly afterwards he went through what he calls a wilderness experience of darkness and doubt. When he knelt to pray "it felt as if God had gone on a journey and heaven was closed." He was in great distress. Early one morning he left his ship and went around the dock to find the vessel of the man who had helped him. He found the ship, went to his friend's cabin, and made known his distress. "What have you been doing wrong?" said the friend. Holmes could not recall any deliberate sin. "Then," said the friend, "as far as I can see, God has been honoring you with a season of good feelings and now He wants you to honor Him by faith." George Holmes says, "I saw it in a minute, turned out the cabin lamp, and departed, having learned a lesson which I have never forgotten—how to walk by Faith" (J. Brice, 9).

Third, remaining steadfast in the Word of God and praying in the Spirit will keep our faith strong and our walk consistent. We will be able to build upon our experiences with God and ensure that our relationship with Him remains genuine. Reading the Bible consistently is a vital key to a vibrant spiritual life. Faith comes by hearing the word of God. Regardless of how much or little we begin reading, the consistency is what feeds our spirit. As we obey the Lord in reading His word, He will grant us the desire to read more. Psalm 37:4 says, "Delight yourself in the Lord and he will give you the desires of your heart." The desires He plants in our hearts make walking in the Spirit a desirable experience. As a result, we will learn proper doctrine and we will not be led astray by every notion that comes along because the Word of God keeps us grounded on a firm foundation of faith and teaching.

Prayer is talking with God and listening to Him. The Baptism with the Holy Spirit enables communication with God to become a reality. We pray and God answers. God uses prayer to give us divine insights. Then we pray accordingly. God wants to talk to us and help us walk with Him throughout the day. This kind of communication is the main reason we have the Holy Spirit given to us, but it is up to us to initiate the praying in the Spirit.

Positive changes will result from praying in the Spirit and reading the Word. Gifts of the Spirit will be recognized in our lives. God will provide the opportunities to discover the gifts of His Spirit and to operate in them. The gifts of the Spirit will affect how we relate with other members of the body of Christ. Because the gifts are in operation all members become influenced in positive, life changing ways. The scripture that commands us to "Let us not give up meeting together, as some are in the habit of doing, but let us encourage one another" (Heb. 10:25) was not given lightly.

Fruit of the Spirit will grow more readily, though not all at once. But noticeably and slowly they will emerge. Fruit of the Spirit will affect our relationships because they will transform our personality. We will become easier to get along with. As we continue to pray in the Spirit with our new language, the Holy Spirit can birth those traits of Himself in us.

After receiving the Baptism with the Holy Spirit, the believers' prayer lives will become more powerful. Their study of God's word will become more meaningful. They will experience His power in witnessing. They will be prepared for spiritual conflict against the world. I John 2:15-17 tells us to stop loving the world and all that it offers, for when we love the world then we don't really love God. They will be prepared for spiritual conflict against the flesh. Galatians 5:16, 17 tells us to obey the Holy Spirit's instructions because He will tell us where to go and what to do. We must stop obeying the desires of our flesh and begin obeying the desires of the Spirit.

We will be prepared for spiritual conflict against the devil himself. Peter warns us to watch out for attacks from Satan, our great enemy, for . . . he's looking for someone to devour (I Peter 5:7-9). Instead, we are to trust the Lord to take us through these temptations. The Holy Spirit within us prepares us for that battle. So after receiving the Baptism with the Holy Spirit, we will experience His power to resist temptation and sin. I Cor. 10:13 tells us that no temptation is irresistible; we can trust God to keep the temptation from becoming too strong to resist. And Paul also tells the Philippians that "I can do everything through Him who gives me strength" (Phil. 4:13).

Receiving the Baptism with the Holy Spirit does not indicate that a believer will become perfect. The Epistles speak of problems within the churches and among individuals. They are full of warnings against sin and calls to holiness in living. These same Epistles were written to people and churches who had experienced the baptizing power of the Holy Spirit. Therefore, we can assume that there was some reason that believers who had received the Baptism with the Holy Spirit still needed such exhortation. There is no indication, scriptural or experiential, that troubles will stop when one receives the Baptism with the Holy Spirit. The very reverse is true actually. Believers can maintain victory only with a constant appropriation of grace and power through a continually renewed fullness of the Spirit and faithful obedience to the Word of God. Being filled with the Holy Spirit is a process—an ongoing action. Continual teaching and prayer and commitment to the Holy Spirit are necessary.

Neither should believers assume that once they are baptized with the Holy Spirit, their lives will be lived on the supernatural plane only. The apostle Paul, obviously blessed with miraculous gifts of the Holy Spirit and obviously filled with the Holy Spirit, suffered hunger and thirst, nakedness, danger, fighting, beatings, imprisonment. When he was shipwrecked, he had to swim to shore under his own power. He also had to help gather sticks for a fire. His life was not marked by exemptions from natural law. However his life was marked because he was not like the world in things of the heart. Power from on high did not transform people into anything other than people with God's power.

The New Testament was written for Christians who need to walk by faith, not by sight, as the normal method of living. Through the Baptism with the Holy Spirit, they have become temples of the living God. God dwells in them and walks in them. But the fellowship of the Lord Almighty is found in separation from all that is unclean and sinful. Daily cleansing from all desires of the flesh will keep the spirit of man clean for God: "Come out from them and be separate, says the Lord. Touch no unclean thing, and I will receive you" (II Cor. 6:17). And Paul adds, "Since we have these promises, ... let us purify ourselves from everything that contaminates body and spirit, perfecting holiness out of reverence for God" (II Cor. 7:1).

The Baptism with the Holy Spirit will bring the Christian new power, new joy, new fellowship, but also new temptations. The newly filled believer will experience the same kind of temptations Christ faced. Jesus faced three temptations in the desert, usually assumed to appeal to the lust of the flesh, the lust of the eyes, and the pride of life.

The first temptation, turning stones to bread, was a temptation to use the newly given power for selfish purposes—to feed himself rather than the multitudes waiting for him. Today's believers are tempted to use the Holy Spirit to gain prominence for themselves in Church meetings, to force themselves to the front so people will notice them. The victory over the temptation of self is to deny the self and the flesh, and renew the walk in the Holy Spirit, focusing attention on Him rather than on ourselves.

The second temptation Christ faced, worshiping Satan, was an offer to give Christ the apparent achievement of His purpose—the world—without going through the cross. We are tempted in the same way when we want to compromise with the spirit of this world and reject the way of our own personal cross. Worldliness must be watched constantly. We are always surrounded with so many things in this world—some of them not sinful in themselves—which would take us away from the plan of God. God's plan is sacrifice and self-surrender. The life of victory over the world comes only through deep worship of the Father in Spirit and truth. This involves full obedience and consecration of all we have, all we are, and all we hope to be.

The third temptation, jumping from the pinnacle of the Temple, was a temptation to become a fanatic or to question God's Word. At times of high pinnacles of spiritual experience, we need to remember to maintain balance. We are on dangerous ground when we reinterpret some of God's Word to fit our own desires or when we adopt an extreme notion just because we see ground for it in one or two isolated texts of the Bible. We have been called to stand on a **Book**, the whole of God's Word, not on a verse or two.

Paul says, "I keep my body under, and bring it into subjection, so that when I preach to others, I won't be a castaway myself" (I Cor. 9:26, 27). Keeping our bodies subjected to the Lord God is not always easy. But we have the power of the Holy Spirit to help us do it. Our responsibility is to use that power and overcome temptations to be selfish and worldly.

God's supreme purpose in giving to man the Holy Spirit is to produce the fruit of the Spirit. Jesus said, "I chose you to go and bear fruit—fruit that will last" (John 15:16). All of the gifts of God given in response to believers' faith are given suddenly. Salvation comes the moment we believe. The Baptism with the Holy Spirit comes as soon as we believe and commit ourselves totally to God. Even the Gifts of the Spirit come suddenly in response to a specific need of the Church body. But the fruit of the Spirit is produced only as we walk with the Spirit day by day, keeping our bodies in subjection and appropriating the divine attributes of Jesus Christ in our lives.

The development of our spiritual selves is the secret of eternal life to come. One day that spiritual self will throw aside all mortality and will stand in the likeness of Jesus Christ Himself. We shall be like Him, for we shall see Him as He is. Let's keep our eyes open and on the goal of living in the Holy Spirit.

Some may be afraid to enter into the life of the Holy Spirit because they are afraid they will fail. Fear is not a part of God's will for believers. Fear is a trick of the enemy to keep believers from entering fully into all that God has for us. Remember the walk in the Spirit is the walk of power. The walk in the Spirit is the walk of peace and joy. Remember, "the kingdom of God is not a matter of eating and drinking, but of righteousness, peace and joy in the Holy

Spirit" (Rom. 14:17).

After being filled with the Holy Spirit, one will experience an entirely new dimension opening up in the Christian life. The initial infilling with the Holy Spirit is only the beginning of a new life in the Lord Jesus Christ. The Holy Spirit fills us with hope and expectation. There will be trials and troubles, of course, but the power of the Holy Spirit will release power, wisdom, and love never before noticed. Even though the power of the evil one may be stronger than ever, we have even stronger power with the Holy Spirit of God (Frost, *Overflowing,* 17). We should make it a habit to begin each day by giving the day back to God and committing ourselves to the Holy Spirit who wants to equip, teach, and use every believer for His glory. Expect something from God every day (Frost, 17).

CHAPTER XIII

USING TONGUES IN PRIVATE PRAYER

When we look at the specific uses for Tongues, we see the necessity of receiving such a gift. One of the main reasons for that necessity is connected to the believers' prayer life. Paul teaches in I Corinthians 14 that both devotional tongues and the gift of tongues are essential to the body of Christ. "Devotional tongues" is *praying in the Spirit in one's private prayer life.* Corporate tongues, where individuals are simultaneously praying in the Spirit, is a vital element of many of today's congregations. And this element of worship is solidly grounded upon an unshakable biblical foundation. Though not all may receive the gift of tongues, which requires an interpretation for corporate edification, all certainly may receive the Holy Spirit and practice devotional tongues in their private prayer life. Using prayer language in corporate prayer is an important part of our worship, but our prayer language may be even more important in our own private times of devotional prayer.

Prayer is not a commodity or a ritual. Prayer is a way of life, a moment-by-moment communion with God. Owen C. Carr reminds us that "Praying in the Spirit is the deepest and most meaningful of all praying. This kind of prayer is available only to the Spirit-filled" (12). The Gospels tell of Jesus' habit of going off alone for times of prayer. Especially before His crucifixion, he went off to pray by Himself. True, he took the three closest disciples with Him "apart to pray," but then He left them and went further off alone (Mark 14:32-35). Our Lord set the example of the source of strength—praying alone and in the Holy Spirit's strength.

Albert L. Hoy, in "Seven Uses of Tongues," shows the importance of using tongues as an important part of our daily prayer language (8-13). Tongues can benefit the Spirit-filled believer in several ways, specifically as

1. A twofold witness. In Acts, when recipients of the Spirit spoke in tongues, the manifestation of tongues was described as the work of the Holy Spirit. In Scripture, the descent of the Holy Spirit upon a person is characterized by supernatural utterance. The Old Testament saints gave witness to the Holy Spirit by prophetic utterance (Num. 11:25, I Sam. 10:10). Speaking in tongues is a sign to unbelievers (I Cor. 14:22).
2. An exalted form of praise. Christians who speak frequently with tongues will realize that their utterances are often praise and thanksgiving to God. The Holy Spirit can praise the Father and the Son as no human language alone can.
3. A fervent type of prayer. Spirit-filled believers receive help in prayer. Paul recommends that believers "pray in the Spirit on all occasions" (Eph. 6:18). Jude also advises believers to "pray in the Holy Spirit" (Jude 20). In private prayer the Christian should use the Holy Spirit's language whenever possible—in the car while driving, at work, in the office, waiting in lines. All these times can be times of blessing as the believer softly to himself and to God speaks in his prayer language.
4. A means of revelation. "Revelation, in the biblical sense, is the unfolding of divine mysteries to the servants of God" (Hoy, "Seven," 11). The mysteries of God are revealed through the Spirit. The Spirit, though, uses supernatural speech to communicate with believers. Tongues are one of the Spirit's ways of communicating with humans.
5. An expression of knowledge. Divine knowledge may come through tongues. Through the Spirit Paul knew that the safety of his fellow travelers required the ship's crew to remain with the vessel (Acts 27:31).

6. An antecedent of prophecy. In Acts 19:6 we are told that the "Holy Spirit came on them and they spoke with tongues and prophesied." Also Old Testament believers, living before Pentecost, prophesied when the Holy Spirit inspired them to do so.

Dennis Bennett, in an article he wrote for *The Charismatic Movement*, describes in some length the value of praying in tongues in one's private devotional time:

> Speaking in tongues enables a person to speak or pray to God without interference from any human source, including himself, without the mind or emotions or will intruding into the picture. The indwelling Spirit says in effect, 'I know what you need to express to God, the Father. Trust me to guide you as you speak.' Thus confession can be made of sins that the mind does not even know about and would not acknowledge, or would soften and rephrase if it did.
>
> . . . love for God can be expressed with a fullness and freedom otherwise impossible to the person because of inhibitions and fears of expression. Intercession can be made for others, expressing their deepest needs, without the intercessor knowing what those needs are (23) (Quoted in Bishop, 13).

Richard Bishop adds that when a believer receives the Baptism in the Holy Spirit, it is a "devotional experience of the deepest dimension" (10). That experience gives the motivation for a continuing devotional life. A personal devotional life is very important for the Spirit-filled Christian. The motivation for this deeper devotional life comes from the believer's awareness of the ministry of the Holy Spirit (Bishop, 13). That awareness comes from the Baptism with the Holy Spirit, accompanied by speaking in other tongues, the language of the Holy Spirit.

The Spirit-filled Christian should use the heavenly gift of tongues liberally in private devotions (Hoy, "Public and Private,"

11). A Christian who has received the Baptism of the Holy Spirit has a divine Teacher within—a Teacher who will lead that Christian into spiritual maturity: "When the Spirit of truth comes, he will guide you into all truth" (John 16:13). In the process of spiritual maturation, speaking in tongues assumes a role of great importance. It is a supernatural utterance, and therefore surpasses any human means of communication and any other means of communion with God (Hoy, "Public and Private," 11). When a believer prays in tongues there is no need to question whether the prayer is heard, for the petition itself is offered to God by the Spirit Himself (Rom. 8:26, 27). If the Spirit offers the petition, the petition must be the will of God. Also, prayer in the Spirit is not open to human misconceptions, for the intercession by the Holy Spirit is always "according to the will of God" (Rom. 8:27).

The contribution to personal spiritual growth is the most important factor in private use of tongues. I Cor 14:4 states that "He who speaks in a tongue edifies himself." Edifying includes the idea of building up or strengthening believers spiritually. Consequently, when we speak in tongues, communing with the Spirit and Father directly, we become "partakers of the divine nature" (2 Peter 1:4). The more Christians are moved by the Spirit to speak with tongues, the more they appropriate the nature of Christ. The spiritual life of the believer depends on the infusion of the divine nature (John 6:53) (Hoy, "Tongues," 11). How better to infuse some of that nature than through the heavenly language given us by the Holy Spirit.

Additionally, the divinely inspired prayer in tongues not only allows the believer to partake of the power of the Holy Spirit, but also allows the Holy Spirit to bring the fruit of the Spirit (Gal 5:22-23) into the life of the believer. The fruit of the Spirit, states Albert Hoy, "is really holiness in behavior, which Paul clearly defines as a continuous development of Christ-likeness by the Holy Spirit within the believer" ("Tongues," 11).

Divine revelations have been imparted privately by the Holy Spirit time after time while the people of God have been in private prayer. Simeon was not publicly informed that he would see the promised Messiah before he died (Luke 2:26). Peter did not have a public word of knowledge or public visionary experience to tell him to go to the house of Cornelius (Acts 10:19, 20). Philip was alone when he went to the desert, so there was no public message for him either (Acts 8:29). John wrote the book of Revelation from an inspiring experience he had when he was alone "in the Spirit on the Lord's day" (Rev. 1:10). Clearly, then, using tongues is important in private devotional prayer as much as or even more than in public worship. The Spirit-filled Christian who desires to grow in grace and in the character of Christ should speak, pray, or even sing in tongues frequently in his daily walk with God.

CHAPTER XIV

CONCLUDING REMARKS

The Holy Spirit is our Comforter. It is a consolation to have His counsel and support. The comfort He brings is more than simple consolation. It is a source of strength which allows us to stand and face life. The word "comfort" also means "encouragement, exhortation, and challenge," according to William Barclay, in *New Testament Words.* In this sense an encourager would put courage into the fainthearted. The whole of the book of Acts illustrates this kind of "comfort" or encouragement. Looked at this way, we can see the Holy Spirit as One who

1. Defends us when we are helpless (Our Defender)
2. Consoles us when we are sorrowful (Our Consoler)
3. Befriends us when we are lonely (Our Friend)
4. Heals us when we are hurt (Our Healer)
5. Refreshes us when we are weary (Our Refresher)
6. Encourages us when we are depressed (Our Encourager)
7. Steadies us when we are uncertain (Our Stabilizer)
8. Strengthens us when we are weak (Our Strengthener)
9. Informs us when we are ignorant (Our Teacher)
10. Steels our soul when we are pressured (Our Reinforcer)
11. Challenges us to be more than conquerors (Our Captain). (Frost, *Set My Spirit*, 47)

"We are *all* meant to be yielded to the work of the Holy Spirit in our lives. We are *all* meant to receive his gifts of power and to receive healing and deliverance in order to serve the body of Christ" (Ranaghan, 64). We are meant to endure persecution and misunderstanding because "the servant is not greater than his master." We must be adaptable and give up our own plans to be used for God's work. We are called to unity—to the task of ecumenism—because the Lord prayed for our unity (Ranaghan, 64). We are all called to serve—whether in a community, a home prayer group, somewhere in the body of Christ. The essence of renewal in the Holy Spirit is not doing grand things for God but "in doing whatever God calls for in a grand way" (65). There is a church to be renewed. There is a pagan world to be evangelized. There is a modern society to be transformed. The face of the earth needs to be changed (65).

Today about 25% of believers from across all denominational lines considers itself Charismatic or Pentecostal. This includes mainline Protestant and Pentecostal denominations, non-denominational churches, independent Charismatic churches, the Orthodox Church, the Roman Catholic Church, and Messianic Jewish synagogues.

If we want to be guided by the Holy Spirit we must walk in the Spirit. To do so, we must live in the Spirit. We cannot expect to live in the Spirit without conflict, for the Holy Spirit is opposite to and opposed to the world of flesh we live in: "For the sinful nature desires what is contrary to the Spirit, and the Spirit what is contrary to the sinful nature. They are in conflict with each other" (Gal. 5:17). We can choose which of the two lives we will lead—the life of the flesh or the life of the Spirit. Actually we do choose to live one or the other because we cannot live both. (Ellis, 145) We cannot be transformed by the Holy Spirit of God and still follow the world. The love of the world and the pride of life and the lusts of the flesh will be cleaned out of us only as we are filled with the Holy Spirit.

Our duty to the Holy Spirit is clear from Eph. 4:30: "And do not grieve the Holy Spirit of God, with whom you were sealed for the day of redemption." Whatever might be in us that would grieve the Holy Spirit must be cleaned out. Until Christians live in a way submitted to the leading of the Holy Spirit, we will look in vain for revival. Let us remember "For God did not call us to be impure, but to live a holy life. Therefore, he who rejects this instruction does not reject man but God, who gives you his Holy Spirit" (I Thess.

4:7). Before the Holy Spirit can fill us or our churches, the temples of our hearts and lives must be cleaned out. "It is not the *kind* of sin that grieves the Holy Spirit," says F. M. Ellis, but rather "sin of *any kind* must grieve him who is himself the essence of holiness" (146). Paul also warned Timothy that "The Spirit clearly says that in later times some will abandon the faith and follow deceiving spirits" (I Tim. 4:1). May we not be among those deceived. Only through the indwelling of the Holy Spirit—His constant presence in us—can we follow Christ in the fullness He intended for us. We pray for more power. Come, Holy Spirit, come. Breathe into every heart your own divine breath. Fill every service with your energy. May the Holy One rest upon His people.

APPENDIX A

HOW TO HELP OTHERS RECEIVE THE BAPTISM WITH THE HOLY SPIRIT

Speaking in tongues is the privilege of each believer. The laying on of hands is instrumental to ensure that believers do speak in tongues. Each of us can help others to receive their prayer language by teaching or praying with them. The following steps may be useful.

1. Study the following passages in a Bible Study: Joel 2:28-29; Mt. 3:11; Lk. 24:49; Jn. 7:37-39; Acts 1:8; Acts 2:1-18; Acts 2:38-39; Acts 8:14-17; Acts 10:44-46; Acts 19:1-7; Rom. 8:9; 1 Cor. 6:19; I Cor. 12:13; I Cor. 14:10,14.
2. Pray and worship God together.
3. Invite them to enter in with you in praying in the Spirit.
4. Remind them that every utterance has meaning with God according to I Cor. 14:10 which says, "Undoubtedly there are all sorts of languages in the world, yet none of them is without meaning."
5. Encourage them to pray in the Spirit daily in their private prayer lives.

APPENDIX B

DATES

Here are the dates of the recorded events in scripture in which believers spoke in tongues: the Day of Pentecost, Acts 2, AD 33; the Samaritans, Acts 8, approx. AD 39; the household of Cornelius, Acts 10, AD 41; the Ephesian men, Acts 19, AD 54; the Corinthian church, 1 Corinthians 14, AD 55; exhortations to be filled with the Spirit, Ephesians 5:18, and to pray in the Spirit, Ephesians 6:18, AD 64; and another exhortation to pray in the Spirit in Jude, verse 20, AD 70.

APPENDIX C

TONGUES FOR TODAY

Scripture indicates that speaking in tongues is the privilege of every believer today, because the evidence of speaking with tongues accompanied the descent of the Holy Spirit. The Bible shows that believers received the baptism with the Holy Spirit and confirmed it by speaking in tongues on many occasions for about 40 years after the Day of Pentecost. It was an experience not only for the disciples and apostles that lived when Christ lived, but, as Peter declared, it was for "you and your children and for all who are far off—for all whom the Lord our God will call" (Acts 2:39).

The record of the Pentecostal Spirit baptism points unmistakably in the direction of being meant for all believers (Schep, 42). We can boldly declare that the baptism with the Spirit is for everyone who believes. This promise is not fulfilled to all believers, because not all have received it, but it is for all those who will receive (43). According to Peter (Acts 2:16 ff.) the promise of the outpouring of the Holy Spirit in the last days had been fulfilled in the Spirit baptism of the 120. "Was that promise intended only for them?" Schep asks. "Most certainly not. It said emphatically that the Spirit baptism was intended for all 'flesh'" (45), which means all mankind. All believing Jews and Gentiles can receive. Peter assures his hearers that this promise is to them, "their children, to all that are far off, everyone whom the Lord our God calls" (44). "Such a Pentecostal Spirit baptism is promised to all who believe in Christ from the Day of Pentecost till the end of the world" (45).

BIBLIOGRAPHY AND RECOMMENDED READING

Barclay, William. *The Gospel of John*, Vol. 2. Philadelphia, PA: Westminster Press, 1975.

Barclay, William. *New Testament Words*. London: SCM Press, 1964.

Barclay, William. *The Promise of the Spirit*. Philadelphia: Westminster Press, 1976.

Barclift, Mark A. "Supernatural Guidance in Acts 16:6-10," *Paraclete* 18, #4 (Fall 1984): 8-10.

Basham, Don. *A Handbook on the Holy Spirit*. Monroeville, PA: Whitaker Books, 1969.

Bennett, Dennis. *Nine 0 'Clock in the Morning*. Plainfield, New Jersey: Logos International, 1970.

Bennett, Dennis. "The Gifts of the Holy Spirit," *The Charismatic Movement*, Michael P. Hamilton, editor. Grand Rapids: Wm. B. Eerdmans Publishing Co., 1975.

Bishop, Richard W. "The Devotional Life," *Paraclete* 13, #3 (Summer 1979): 10-13.

Blumhofer, Edith L. *Pentecost in My Soul*. Springfield, MO: Gospel Publishing House, 1989.

Boyd, Frank M. *The Spirit Works Today*. Springfield: Gospel Publishing House, 1970.

Brandt, R. L. "The Case for Speaking with Other Tongues," *Pentecostal Evangel*, 48 (June 5, 1960): 4.

Brice, J. *Pentecost*. Quoted in *Paraclete* 17, #1 (Winter 1983): 9.

Bright, Bill. *The Holy Spirit: the Key to Supernatural Living*. San Bernardino, CA: Here's Life Publishers, Inc., 1980.

Bruner, Frederick Dale. *A Theology of the Holy Spirit: The Pentecostal Experience and the New Testament Witness.* Grand Rapids: Wm. B. Eerdmans Pub., 1970.

Bundrick, David R. "New Testament Fulfillment of Anointing," *Paraclete* 19, #3 (Summer 1985): 15-18.

Carlson, G. Raymond. "This Is That," *Paraclete* 8, #2 (Spring 1974): 22-25.

Carr, Owen C. "Praying in the Spirit," *Paraclete* 12, #3 (Summer 1978): 12-16.

Chadwick, Samuel. "The Way to Pentecost," *Paraclete* 16, #1 (Winter 1982): 30.

Christiansen, Larry. *Speaking In Tongues and its Significance for the Church.* London: Fountain Trust, 1968.

Conner, Walter Thomas. *The Work of the Holy Spirit: A Treatment of the Biblical Doctrine of the Divine Spirit.* Nashville: Broadman Press, 1949.

Duffield, Guy P. and Nathaniel M. Van Cleave. *Foundations of Pentecostal Theology*. Los Angeles: L.I.F.E. Bible College, 1983.

Du Plessis, David. *The Spirit Bade Me Go.* Plainfield, NJ: Logos International, 1970.

Durasoff, Steve. *Bright Wind of the Spirit: Pentecostalism Today*. Tulsa, OK: RHEMA Bible Church, 1972.

Ellis, F. M. "The Holy Spirit and the Christian," *The Person and Ministry of the Holy Spirit,* ed. A. C. Dixon. New York: Garland Pub. Inc., 45 vols., 1880-1950.

Ford, Charles W. "The Holy Spirit and Christian Growth," *Paraclete* 18, #2 (Spring 1984): 7-9.

Ford, Charles W. "Walking in the Spirit," *Paraclete* 16, #1 (Winter 1982):19-21.

Frost, Robert C. *Overflowing Life*. Plainfield, NJ: Logos International, 1971.

Frost, Robert C. *Set My Spirit Free*. Plainfield, NJ: Logos International, 1973.

Gannon, T. E. "They Were All Filled," *Paraclete* 6, #3 (Summer

1972): 23-26.

Gee, Donald. *All With One Accord.* Springfield, MO: Gospel Publishing House, 1961.

Gee, Donald. 1955 Pentecostal World Conference speech, printed in *Pentecost,* #34 (Dec. 1955): 10.

Gee, Donald. *Pentecost,* No. 25 (Sept. 1953): 17.

Goforth, Jonathan. *By My Spirit.* Quoted in Ralph Riggs, *The Spirit Himself.* Springfield, MO: Gospel Publishing House, 1949.

Graves, Arthur H. "How to Receive the Baptism." *Paraclete* 16, #1 (Winter 1982): 8-12.

Graves, Robert W. "Praying in Tongues," *Paraclete* 20, #4 (Fall 1986): 14-15.

Hamill, James E. "The Pentecostal Experience," *Paraclete* 14, #2 (Spring 1980): 1-3.

Heron, Alasdair I. C. *The Holy Spirit.* Philadelphia: Westminster Press, 1983.

Holdcroft, L. Thomas. "Receiving the Baptism in the Holy Spirit," *Paraclete* 14, #1 (Winter 1980): 4-7.

Hollenweger, Walter J. *The Pentecostals.* Peabody, Mass: Hendrickson Publishers, 1972.

Holmes, George E. "The Ministries of Christ and the Holy Spirit," *Paraclete* 17, #4 (Fall 1983): 15-19.

Horton, Harold. *Baptism in the Holy Spirit: A Challenge to the Whole-hearted Seekers After God.* London: Assembly of God Publishing House, 1956.

Horton, Harold. *The Gifts of the Spirit.* 5th ed. Springfield, MO: Gospel Publishing House, 1953.

Hoy, Albert L. "Public and Private Uses of the Gift of Tongues," *Paraclete* 2, #4 (Fall 1968): 10-14.

Hoy, Albert L. "Regeneration," *Paraclete* 15, #1 (Winter 1981): 14-17.

Hoy, Albert L. "Seven Uses of Tongues," *Paraclete* 13, #2 (Spring 1979): 8-13.

Hoy, Albert L. "The Spirit of Christ" *Paraclete* 16, #2 (Spring 1982): 23-27.

Hoy, Albert L. "The Spirit of Sonship," *Paraclete* 6, #3 (Summer 1972): 8-12.

Hoy, Albert L. "Tongues and Spiritual Development," *Paraclete* 14, #3 (Summer 1980): 10-14.

Humphries, A. L. *The Holy Spirit in Faith and Experience.*

Hunter, Charles and Frances. *Two Sides of a Coin.* Old Tappan, NJ: Fleming H. Revell Co., 1973.

Jorstad, Erling, ed. *The Holy Spirit in Today's Church: A Handbook of the New Pentecostalism.* New York: Abingdon Press, 1973.

Kelsey, Morton. *Tongue Speaking: An Experiment in Spiritual Experience.* New York: Crossroad, 1964.

Lampe, G.W.H. "Holy Spirit," *The Interpreters' Dictionary of the Bible.* Nashville: Abingdon Press, 1962.

Lampe, G. W. H. *The Seal of the Spirit: A study in the Doctrine of Baptism and Confirmation in the New Testament and the Fathers.* London: SPCK, 1967.

Lancaster, John. "But the Holy Ghost said 'Yes'," *Paraclete* 15, #1 (Winter 1981): 22-25.

Lancaster, John. "The Life-Style of the Spirit," *Paraclete* 13, #2 (Spring 1979): 4-7.

Lancaster, John. "The Transforming Spirit," *Paraclete* 16, #1 (Winter 1982): 22-27.

Lastinger, A. L. "The Holy Spirit in the Old Testament," *Paraclete* 16, #2 (Spring 1982): 13-15.

Lastinger, A. L. "The Parakletos: Our Holy Ally," *Paraclete* 18, #32 (Spring 1984): 1-2.

Lawson, J. Gilchrist. *Paraclete* 16, #1 (Winter 1982): 7.

Linzey, James F. *The Holy Spirit.* Fairfax, VA: Xulon Press, 2004.

McIntire, James R. *The Life of the Holy Spirit.* St. Louis, MO: Bethany Press, 1930.

Millard, Amos D. "Humanism and the Holy Spirit," *Paraclete* 16, #1 (Winter 1982): 5-7.

Mooth, Verla A. *The Age of the Spirit.* Pecos: Dove Publications, 1972.

Nelson, P. C. *The Baptism in the Spirit.* Enid, OK: Southwestern Press, 1939.

Orchard, R. E. "The Holy Spirit and This Age," *Paraclete* 15, #1 (Winter 1981): 5-8.

Otis, George. *High Adventure.* Old Tappan, NJ: Fleming H. Revell Co, 1971.

Pache, Rene. *The Person and Work of the Holy Spirit.* Trans. J. D. Emerson. Chicago: Moody Press, 1954.

Parsons, Arthur H. "The Personality of the Holy Spirit" *Paraclete* 15, #4 (Fall 1981):8-10.

Pearlman, Myer. *Knowing the Doctrines of the Bible.* Springfield, MO: Gospel Pub. House, 1939.

Pulkington, Graham. *Gathered for Power.* New York: Morehouse-Barlow Co, 1972.

Ranaghan, Kevin and Dorothy. *Catholic Pentecostals Today.* South Bend, Indiana: Charismatic Renewal Services, 1983.

Rice, Frank B. "Practical Implication of Terms Describing the Baptism in the Holy Spirit" *Paraclete* 3, #1 (Winter 1969): 7-10.

Riggs, Ralph. *The Spirit Himself.* Springfield, MO: Gospel Publishing House, 1949.

Ryrie, Charles Caldwell. *The Holy Spirit.* Chicago: Moody Bible Institute, 1965.

Schep, John A. *Baptism in the Spirit According to Scripture.* Plainfield, NJ: Logos International, 1972.

Sherrill, John. *They Speak With Other Tongues.* New York: McGraw-Hill, 1964.

Stott, John R. W. *Baptism and Fullness of the Holy Spirit.* Downer's Grove, Ill.: Intervarsity Press, 1964.

Swete, Henry Barclay. "The Holy Spirit," article in *Hastings Bible Dictionary.*

Swete, Henry Barclay. *The Holy Spirit in the New Testament.* Grand Rapids: Baker Book House (c. 1910), 1976.

Thomas, W. H. Griffith. *The Holy Spirit of God.* Grand Rapids: Eerdman's, 1972.

Torrey, R. A. *The Baptism with the Holy Spirit.* Minneapolis, MN: Dimension Books, 1972.

Torrey, R. A. *The Person and Work of the Holy Spirit.* New York: Fleming H. Revell, 1910.

Walvoord, John F. *The Holy Spirit.* Grand Rapids, MI.: Zondervan Pub. House, 1972.

Ward, Wayne E. *Layman's Library of Christian Doctrine: The Holy Spirit*. Nashville, TN: Broadman Press, 1987.
Warfield, *Presbyterian and Reformed Review*, Vol. VI. P. 687.

Printed in the United States
42158LVS00008B/169-183